KNITS
for
BOYS

**27 Patterns
for Little Men**

· · · · · · · · + · · · · · · ·

**Grow-with-Me
Tips & Tricks**

KATE OATES
Photography by Sara Parker

STACKPOLE
BOOKS

D1229533

0 11557 01361 0

This book is dedicated to my four precious little men.

• •

Published by
STACKPOLE BOOKS
5067 Ritter Road
Mechanicsburg, PA 17055
www.stackpolebooks.com

Printed in the United States of America

10 9 8 7 6 5 4 3 2 1

First edition

Cover design by Tessa J. Sweigert
Photography by Sara Parker
Schematics by Caroline Stover
Illustrations on pages 2 and 3 by Jill Zielinski Designs

Library of Congress Cataloging-in-Publication Data

Oates, Kate.
  Knits for boys : 27 patterns for little men + grow-with-me tips & tricks /
Kate Oates ; photography by Sara Parker.
    pages cm
  Includes index.
  ISBN 978-0-8117-1361-0
  1. Knitting—Patterns. 2. Boys' clothing. I. Title.
  TT825.O2285 2015
  746.43'2—dc23
                                                    2014040209

Table of Contents

Introduction

This is a book all about knitting for boys. It is a collection of classic designs with a modern edge here and a whimsical touch there. The designs are geared for those knitting for boys ages four to twelve, a charming spot between baby and teenager, but the extras in this book make it a must-have for anyone who knits for children. The goal of this collection is to blow our little men away with designs that are created just for them.

Every child is unique and has his own style and preferences, and the various designs and options in this book give you plenty of ways to create knits your boys will want to wear. The projects range from sweaters to caps to accessories like suspenders and a belt. They are stylish and modern, boyish but grown up enough for pre-teens. Color choices range from happy brights to bold neutrals. These color options, matched with a fresh take on cables and colorwork, set a new timeless standard on what boys will really want to wear. Beginning knitters will find plenty of projects to choose from to get their feet wet, but knitters at all experience levels will find entertainment and challenge among the variety of projects and options. Follow the four basic steps below to customize knits just right for the boys in your life.

Step One

FLATTER THEM WITH FIT

The one problem with knitting for children is how quickly they grow out of your knits. It's a challenge to make knits that will fit for two to three seasons while looking good in each. This book features a "Grow-with-Me" theme to make your knits wearable for more than one year, and includes a reference section that discusses children's growth patterns. I then use that growth-pattern information to present practical strategies for project planning to help you ensure your child gets more wear out of each knitted garment. This section walks knitters through a little necessary math to make adjustments in patterns and explains how schematics are to be interpreted. The accompanying Grow-with-Me section of patterns includes designs with features that have already made sleeve and hem length adjustable in a variety of ways.

Step Two

TEMPT THEM WITH TEXTURE

Whether it's cabling or simply a combination of knits and purls, texture adds intrigue and depth. One of my sons is particularly tactile and his favorite thing about my knitting projects is touching them. He loves the feel of his cabled sweater. The Touch-Me Texture designs are also for the classically inclined—textural knits are unendingly stylish. These designs also grow up very well; knitters will be tempted to size them up for an older child (or, ahem, themselves) or perhaps to make daddy a matching sweater.

Step Three

CAPTIVATE THEM WITH COLOR

My oldest son loves colors, patterns, and any combination thereof. The designs in the Color Collection are adventurous and range from cute to quirky. They include stranded colorwork, intarsia motifs that are playful yet grown up enough for tweens, striping, and tastefully contrasting cuffs and hems.

Step Four

OFFER THEM OPTIONS

The Grow-with-Me Sizing and Styling reference section in the front of the book provides many options for sizing customization. It also includes the necessary reference tools to make substantive changes to a design like adding a textural stitch pattern or colorwork, or adding any of several pocket styles or a hood. Not only do boys love to be knitted for, but there is an infinite number of ways to make a project perfect for its recipient. I hate hearing from knitters that their boys "will not wear anything they knit." With some attention to detail, this can be overcome.

Grow-with-Me Sizing and Styling

Sizing and Schematics

Every sized knitting pattern is based on one thing: the listed gauge. Perhaps you have been knitting for a while but you still consider "gauge" a dirty word. To the contrary—gauge is a fabulous and useful tool, but if ignored, you may spend hours and hours knitting a beautiful sweater just for it to be too small for the recipient.

Getting Gauge

Gauge simply refers to the number of stitches and the number of rows in a given area. In this book, gauges are listed over a 4-inch/10 cm square area. If the area is smaller than 4 inches, you're told how wide the actual stitch count should measure. For example, the Brothers' Belt is less than 4 inches wide, so the gauge for that pattern tells you that your 12-stitch cast-on should measure approximately 2 inches.

WORKING A GAUGE SWATCH

You'll want to knit up a gauge swatch every time you are preparing to knit a sized project. Cast on enough stitches so that your finished swatch measures at least 5 inches square. For the most accurate gauge measurement, you'll want to be able to measure 4 inches worth of stitches, horizontally and vertically, without including any selvedge edge (outside stitches) in the measurement. Selvedge stitches are generally much looser than those toward the middle of your knitting, so they can really throw off a gauge measurement. Once you have cast on, pay attention to the stitch pattern you're to use for the swatch and which needle size to use in the case where more than one is called for in the pattern. Many projects will have a hem or cuffs worked in a smaller needle size than the main body of the work, so you'll want to use the correct needle size as indicated for your swatch. Similarly, if a stitch pattern is used for the majority of the design, you should be provided a gauge measurement in that stitch pattern instead of in stockinette stitch. Your gauge can really change when you are working both knits and purls on the same row or working in a cabled pattern, so it's very important to use these stitch patterns in your swatch. The idea behind a swatch is to mimic your actual knitting project as closely as possible. For this reason, if you are working a piece in the round, you should also swatch in the round (see next section for instructions).

Once you have completed knitting your swatch, bind off and block your swatch, following the directions on page 3.

Depending on the fiber you use, blocking may alter gauge significantly.

Swatching In the Round

Many knitters have different tension when knitting in the round versus back and forth because they tend to purl more loosely than they knit. If you are working stockinette in the round, there is no purling at all so your gauge is likely to be tighter than a back and forth swatch would yield. This can be a problem no matter who you are knitting for, but even more of an issue for a growing child since you know they will only be getting bigger. A tighter gauge means that your project will end up being smaller than the pattern intends. Follow the steps below to swatch "in the round" and avoid this issue.

1. With a single double-pointed needle (DPN), cast on an appropriate number of stitches for a swatch at least 6 inches wide. Note that this is a larger area than suggested for a back-and-forth swatch. In this particular swatching technique, the outside stitches will be even looser than they normally are.

2. With a second DPN, knit across the first row of stitches and *do not turn*.

3. Slide stitches to the right-hand side of your DPN, ready to be worked again on the knit side.

4. Pull the working yarn around the back of the work *very* loosely.

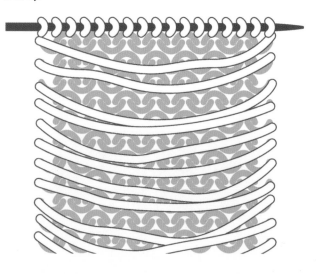

5. Repeat steps 2–4 until your swatch measures at least 5 inches from the cast-on edge.

6. Bind off all stitches, break yarn, and weave the end through the last stitch.

7. Turn your swatch over, and very carefully cut through the middle of the loose strands of yarn on the wrong side.

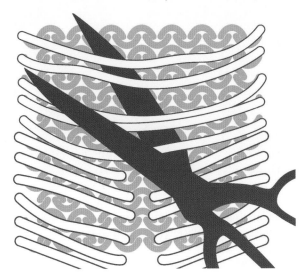

8. If you are working with an animal fiber that is bouncy and holds (merino, alpaca), you can gently block the swatch as is without fear of it coming apart. However, if you are working with an acrylic fiber or something otherwise slippery, you'll need to secure the swatch before blocking. Simply tie the strands together two to four at a time on each side. Remember that you only need 4 inches of measuring fabric on the inside, so it is fine and expected for your outside stitches to be a bit wonky.

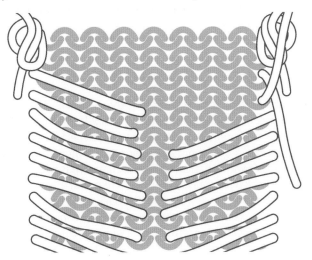

9. Block.

10. Take your measurements from the center 4 inches of your swatch.

BLOCKING

There are a couple of different but equally valid methods of blocking. I use them both depending on the project. Primarily, I wet block my knits. Wet blocking describes the process of immersing your project in water, letting it soak, and then laying it out to dry. You might also choose to use a rinseless wash like Eucalan or Soak. After your project has soaked for several minutes, use a towel (or several) to gently blot the garment and get out the excess water to speed up your drying time. Once it is no longer dripping, gently tug on each section of the garment to even out the stitches. Place a dry towel on a flat surface, then lay out the garment carefully, smoothing it down and straightening edges. Pat the garment into place using the schematic from the design to determine each section's measurement. For children's garments, I do not generally bother with using pins; however, using them will certainly not hurt.

The other type of blocking is steam blocking. If you are having a difficult time getting an edge to lie flat, steam blocking is your best bet. Use an iron on a setting appropriate for the yarn's fiber content (based on the yarn label), place a towel or sheet in between your garment and the iron, and gently press your knit. The steam should relax the fibers and you can tug on them in the same manner as you would during a wet block. Just be very careful not to burn your sweater!

NEEDLE SIZES

Patterns usually list a suggested needle size. However, the important thing is not that you use the suggested needle size, but that you end up with the same gauge. Needle sizes are *only* suggestions, and they should be utilized just as a starting point for your swatch. If a pattern calls for multiple needle sizes, adjust the other needle sizes up or down as necessary so that there is the same gap between larger and smaller needle sizes as is called for. For example, if the pattern calls for sizes 6 and 7 needles but you need to use size 9 needles to get the gauge as for the size 7 needle, then you should end up using sizes 8 and 9.

Fit

Because kids come in all shapes and sizes, all the patterns in this book include both a standard size and relevant measurement notation for sizing. The sizes are based on a standard child's size chart. If you're knitting for a child that isn't available for measurement, you should feel confident knitting based on the listed sizes in the same way you would purchasing something from a store. However, if the child is available for measurement, it is always safer to take some measurements and use them to choose a size. Averages are great guidelines, but just as every adult is not an average size medium, every child is not necessarily the average size for their age. Measurements can also be very helpful when the child seems to be between sizes.

Child Sizing Chart*

Child's Size	4	6	8	10	12
Chest (in.)	23	25	26.5	28	30
(cm)	58.5	63.5	67	71	76
Center Back Neck-to-Cuff (in.)	19.5	20.5	22	24	26
(cm)	49.5	52	56	61	66
Back Waist Length (in.)	9.5	10.5	12.5	14	15
(cm)	24	26.5	31.5	35.5	38
Cross Back (Shoulder to Shoulder) (in.)	9.75	10.25	10.75	11.25	12
(cm)	25	26	27	28.5	30.5
Sleeve Length to Underarm (in.)	10.5	11.5	12.5	13.5	15
(cm)	26.5	29	31.5	34.5	38

* Based on Standards & Guidelines for Crochet and Knitting, Yarn Craft Council of America

Ease

"Ease" refers to how tightly or loosely the finished garment should fit on the body. If an item suggests "negative ease," this means the garment should measure smaller than the actual child. Conversely, an item sized with "positive ease" should end up larger than the child. If an item has "no ease" this means it should come out to be very close to or the same as the size of the child. Patterns include notation on what size is being modeled and how the item is intended to fit. For boys, most clothing is sized with positive ease but there are a few exceptions, such as hats and socks.

Schematic Basics

For every clothing pattern, the conscientious designer provides a basic line drawing with detailed measurements of each of the various pieces to the garment. This drawing is referred to as a schematic and it is one of the most important tools you have as a knitter for making your project fit. Understanding each of these measurements is necessary to make the best use of the schematic. Schematics are less useful for accessories like hats and scarves since they have only a couple of components. This section focuses on tops, which are tricky to fit while also the most popular garment to knit.

Each schematic measurement can either be categorized as a width measurement or a length measurement. Generally, circumference and other width measurements should account for ease, whereas length measurements should be the same as the child's actual measurements. Added length is not described as ease. In this section, we will look at each measurement separately to discuss how it should be interpreted, especially in relationship to ease and fit. Measure-ment labels are fairly straightforward, but measuring in the wrong spot can really interfere with your fit.

WIDTH MEASUREMENTS

Neck Circumference

This measurement describes the finished circumference of the neckline. It is most important for crewnecks or other necklines that are closed. The circumference must be large enough that it stretches over the head and doesn't make the wearer feel choked by their garment, but not so large that the sweater falls off the shoulders or looks oddly low-cut in the front (especially for boys!). Usually this number falls about halfway between the head circumference and the actual neck circumference. Children's garments need a larger proportional neck circumference than do adult gar-ments since kids' head sizes are commonly disproportional to their neck sizes.

Back Neck

Usually you will be provided with either a back neck or a neck circumference measurement but not both. A circum-ference measurement will include the back neck in its cal-culation. Back neck is not a circular measurement but instead is a width. If the neckline in a garment is not circu-lar, the back neck measurement is more useful than a non-round circumference would be. The back neck can be estimated as one third of the cross back (described below). Like neck circumference, back neck widths are usually larger proportionally in designs for kids than in those for adults.

Cross Back

This is a measurement you'll see primarily in designs with set-in sleeves. This is the area between the shoulder blades.

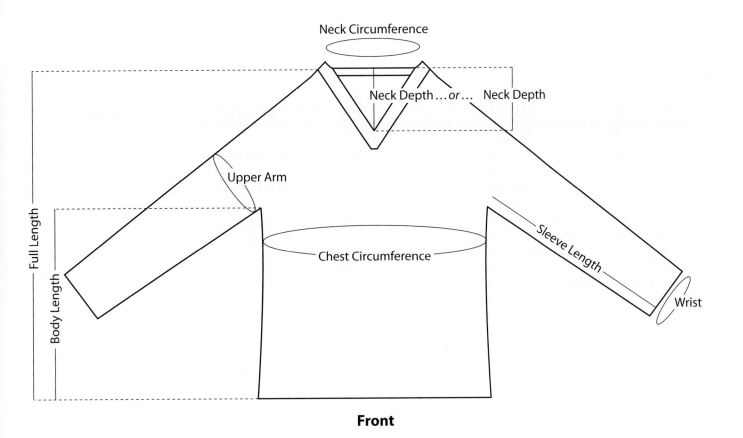

Front

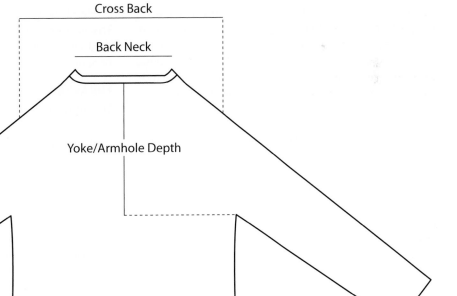

Back

Sample schematics labeling measurements as they will appear on schematics throughout the book.

For the best fit, you want this measurement to be actual. Shoulders will hang awkwardly if the back width is too large.

Chest/Waist/Hip

A pattern may have just one of these or all three, depending on shaping. For most kids' garments, including those in this book, shaping is unnecessary, which means you will only be provided with a chest measurement. This should be a full circumference measurement and it is usually the primary measurement to consider when deciding what size to knit because it is the measurement on which all others are based. The largest amount of ease in an unshaped sweater should occur at the chest. For fitted-against-the-body sweaters, you should shoot for an inch or less of positive ease. For pullovers or cardigans that would have layers worn underneath, 1.5 to 3 inches is a better bet. Kids don't usually like their clothing to be tight. For cardigans, a finished chest measurement of the buttoned or otherwise closed sweater is provided. To measure your child's chest, run the tape measure all the way around his body right underneath the armpits. This is the widest part of the chest.

Upper Arm

This measurement describes the widest part of the upper arm. It should be based on the number of stitches at the very top of the sleeve. The upper arm should have 50 to 75 percent as much ease as the chest. If the chest circumference is 2 inches larger than the actual chest, the upper arm should be in the range of 1 to 1.5 inches larger than the actual arm at its widest. When rounding this number, round up—kids need to be able to move. At the same time, a too-large sleeve will get in the way, so don't overestimate.

Wrist/Cuff

This is the narrowest part of the sleeve. In most cases, your target measurement should be slightly larger than the actual wrist, but with less ease than for the upper arm. If it is too large, a longer sleeve will come down and cover the hand. A smaller wrist will hold a bit of extra length within the forearm of the sleeve.

LENGTH MEASUREMENTS

Neck Depth

This is a measurement for the *front* of the sweater only. It will tell you how much lower the front neckline is than the back neckline. It is important to note if you decide you want to adjust how low the collar goes.

Yoke/Armhole Depth

In a raglan design, or circular yoke, you'll see a yoke measurement. In a set-in sleeve or other seamed piece, you're more likely to see armhole depth. These two measurements are really describing the same thing: the area where the top of the sleeve meets the body. Both should be measured straight down from the center back neckline when working from the top down and from the underarm straight up when working bottom-up. Ease is not added into this measurement, and it is very stable even amidst a variety of different styles.

Sleeve Length

This is the sleeve measurement beginning at the underarm to the cuff. Sometimes the cuff is included in this measurement; other times it is written separately. Take note as to which is the case and add the two measurements together if necessary. Ease is not added to sleeve length.

Body Length

This measures the body from the end of the yoke/armhole depth to bottom. Like the sleeve length measurement, take note of whether the garment's hem is included or not.

Full Length

The full length of the garment is the total length from neckline to hem. If a pattern does not provide you with this measurement, you should be able to calculate it easily by adding the armhole depth/yoke to the body length.

Using each piece of a schematic is like putting together a puzzle. Knowing how the pieces fit together will help you to make adjustments and decisions about how to personalize the fit of your knits. When knitting for growing children, understanding how they grow is the next step to creating a garment with maximum longevity.

How Kids Grow: Growth Patterns

No one has to tell you that kids grow fast. Do you normally try to knit several sizes larger in order to have something they can grow into later? This solution is certainly valid but I argue that there is a better way. If you understand how and where in their bodies kids are really growing, you can work up a garment that not only fits for several seasons, but doesn't necessarily look oversized for those first couple of years. It's the best of both worlds.

Up Not Out

The golden rule of kids' growth (aside from "every child is different"—how many times have you heard that sentiment?) is that for most of them, *they grow taller and more long limbed much faster than they grow in circumference.*

The first year of life holds an astounding rate of growth. Babies tend to get a full one-third taller during that first year. Fortunately, they are teensy at that age and so knitting for them goes quickly. During year two, they are likely to grow another 5 inches or so, which is half as much as during year one. Once they hit those terrible twos, growth

stabilizes a bit and children grow approximately 2 to 2.5 inches taller every year until puberty. Research has also shown that growth spurts are more likely to occur in the summertime than in the fall and winter.[1,2]

Once puberty hits, the averages go out the window and boys can top off with a full foot over just a few years. Boys enter puberty later than girls and this adolescent growth spurt doesn't start until age twelve or later. For the size range in this book, I focus on that 2 to 2.5 inch average per year to give patterns some growing room.

Sure, these kids are growing around the chest, too! But this growth is simply not as noticeable from year to year as is the growth in height. Also, the built-in ease in a garment already adds growing room around the chest. If a sweater is initially 2.5 inches larger than the actual chest circumference, there is already some room for kid expansion around the middle.

1. "Patterns of Growth," Human Growth Foundation. June 2014.
   http://www.hgfound.org/pub_patterns.asp
2. "Your Child's Growth," Kids Health. June 2014.
   http://kidshealth.org/parent/growth/growing/childs_growth.html

Knitterly Math: Making Adjustments for the Perfect Fit

Now that you know how to interpret a schematic and that the length areas are those in which we should be most concerned for growing kids, the following section will detail the steps to take in a pattern for making your own adjustments. I'll first describe my suggestions on where *not* to make pattern changes if you are new to knitterly math, and then provide you with some worksheets for the areas that are most customizable. Of course, any pieces can be changed and made to work, but some areas are simply easier to adjust than others. Note that my suggestions refer to altering pieces of the design or the sizing, but not the whole. If you are adding a size to an existing design, it will be necessary to work out the changes to every component and not just some components.

What Not to Change

Chest Circumference

The finished chest is usually the centerpiece of the design from which all the other pieces are built. If you adjust this number significantly without truly knowing the mechanics behind the design, there is a good chance that you will throw off the proportions of the design. The chest size should guide your choice of size.

Yoke/Armhole Depth

In a raglan-style sweater design, shaping is worked in between the four main sections of the sweater: the front, a sleeve, the back, and the second sleeve. This shaping is either increasing or decreasing at a steady rate depending on whether the design is worked top-down or bottom-up. Although adding length below the increases/decreases (toward the underarm area, not the neckline) can be done quite easily by knitting extra rows/rounds, adjusting in the raglan shaping area risks disrupting the flow and look of the seams. This measurement is also very stable with chest size. For every 2 inches increased in chest size, only .25 to .5 inches needs to be added to the armhole depth. Kids are growing in their body length more so than they are growing in the armhole. My personal philosophy is to design patterns top-down unless there is a component to the design (certain stitch patterns, for example) that makes decreasing at the yoke preferable to increasing. This way,

after the yoke increases are completed, the sweater can actually be tried on before the sleeves are separated. If you must adjust the length of the yoke, do not do it amidst the shaping, but instead do it toward the underarm. Adding length at the neck when the stitch count, and thus circumference, is the smallest will result in fabric that is unpleasantly stretched, whereas adding length at the underarm, where the circumference is at its largest, will drape nicely and work with the finished chest measurement.

Cross Back

Like armhole depth, this measurement is very stable and really coincides well with the finished chest measurement. In a set-in sleeves design, the number of stitches in the cross back usually correlates with the number of stitches in the shoulder. If you adjust one, you'll need to adjust the other.

Tailor-Made: Easy Adjustments

Many adjustments are really quite straightforward and easy. However, when a pattern is complex either because it contains a stitch pattern or has shaping, there is some easy math you can compute in order to make your results well planned and truer to the design's original aesthetic. The worksheets on the following pages can be utilized in various areas of the garment. I'll talk more specifically about how to use them for each piece of the garment as we once again walk through each piece of the schematic.

USING LIFELINES

The suggestions here for adjusting various schematics are described as though you planned the changes ahead of time. This is optimal, but sometimes you may not realize you have a sizing issue until after you see the garment on its new owner. Rest assured that in most cases things can be fixed and it doesn't have to be stressful. I suggest that before doing significant ripping or pulling out rows/rounds backward (ripping out from the cast-on edge down, for example, if you need to adjust the neckline on a top-down garment), place a just-in-case lifeline in your work first.

Here's how:

1. Thread a tapestry needle with scrap yarn.

2. Place the garment on a flat surface with lots of light so that you can best see your individual stitches.

3. Identify your starting point: For pieces worked flat, start at one end of the work. For pieces worked in the round, if you can see the jog (where you move from one round to the next), start at the beginning of the round. If you cannot find the jog, choose a spot in the underarm or back area.

4. Weave the needle and yarn through only *one* leg of each stitch through the entire row, being very careful to stay in the same row.

5. Pull the yarn so that there is plenty of length on either end.

6. Fearlessly rip back or cut out above/below your lifeline. It will keep the rest of your knitting safe while you make your adjustments!

Keep this tool in your arsenal as you read through the following sections.

ADJUSTING CIRCUMFERENCE

Stitch Adjustment Worksheet— Width/Circumference

A = ___ stitches per 4 inches in gauge swatch

B = A/4 = ___ stitches per 1 inch
(do not round this number)

C = ___ desired width/circumference in inches

D = B x C = ___ desired number of total stitches

E = ___ stitches in pattern

F = D - E = ___ additional stitches

Neck Circumference, Back Neck, and Collar

A knitter's nightmare! The sweater is complete and blocked and beautiful and is presented to its little one and then...it won't fit over his head. It has happened to me, and if you've knit for babies or children it's probably happened to you a time or two as well. Do not panic. We can fix this with just a little effort.

Should you decide that a collar is too tight, adjusting the neckline is totally doable. There are several different ways to accomplish this. The most straightforward way is to simply pick up more stitches for the collar. Usually there are some neckline shaping rows in the front. You can pick up 1 stitch

for every row in the neckline shaping, though most patterns are written to suggest that you only pick up a ratio of about 3 stitches to every 4 rows—this is why you have a little wiggle room. Depending on the gauge of the design and the neck depth, sometimes you can add a full inch to the neckline by just picking up a couple of stitches more on either side. So if things are just a smidge too tight, try this first.

If you need to go a bit deeper and add even more room, you can eliminate a shaping row at the neckline, which will provide for at least 8 more stitches in a raglan design. To do this in a top-down design, you'll cast on an additional 8 stitches (2 in each section) and work one fewer increase rows. If working bottom-up, you'll skip the very last decrease. If the project is completed, use lifelines to pull out one or two rows at the top of the sweater.

If you want to alter the neckline by more than this single row, look to adjust only the stitches in the back neck. Again, make your alterations at the top of the sweater and adjust the number of shaping rows to accommodate your desired back neck number; fewer shaping rows are worked just over the back section.

One final neckline option is to adjust the neck depth. Adjustment of this measurement is covered in the Adjusting Length section. The depth is related to the overall neckline circumference but the measurement itself is vertical and row-related, and thus I've detailed it separately. If you add more depth in the front of the sweater, you will simultaneously enlarge the circumference.

Since a standard neckline is fairly small, an inch or two of adjustment is usually all you need. But if you would like to be precise, you can use the Stitch Adjustment Worksheet to determine how many additional stitches you would like to add. If you do this, I suggest measuring the neckline of an existing garment, one which you know has a good fit. Use this as your number for C on the worksheet and fill it out the rest of the way according to your gauge swatch. Just remember to make sure that you adjust your final number F to work with the multiple in your stitch pattern, if applicable. You can reference the next section for an example of this worksheet filled out and how to adjust this final number to suit.

Upper Arm

In adult designs, the upper arm can be a tricky spot because our arms really do vary in circumference and are not necessarily proportional to finished chest size. I have not typically found this to be the case for young children, but it does happen. It should not be necessary to size down an upper arm, because a little bit of extra ease should not be a problem. However, if you have a child who prefers a looser sleeve or has a larger upper arm proportionally, adding a few extra stitches can be a great fix. Use the Stitch Adjustment Worksheet in order to determine how many stitches you need to add.

Once you have determined how many additional stitches you would like to have in your upper arm, consider the stitch pattern. If there is a necessary multiple for this pattern, adjust your number of stitches up or down as appropriate to land within it.

Next, decide where to add these stitches. There are two good choices. One is within the neckline stitches and the other would be underneath the raglan stitches toward the underarm. The easiest place to add stitches is at the neckline. However, consider that you will be adding the stitches in both sleeves and you do not want to end up with a gapingly large neckline. If you are adding more than a couple of stitches to each arm, I suggest working additional row/round(s) of raglan shaping on the underarm side and only work increases or decreases in the arm section during this round(s). You might also combine both approaches.

The example below shows a completed worksheet. Afterward, I walk you through the final decision-making steps and describe the options mentioned above as they relate to the example.

Stitch Adjustment Worksheet Example

A = 20 stitches per 4 inches in gauge swatch
B = 20/4 = 5 stitches per 1 inch
C = 9.5 = desired circumference in inches
D = 5 x 9.5 = 47.5 desired number of total stitches
E = 44 = stitches in pattern
F = 47.5 - 44 = 3.75 additional stitches

In this example, there is a stitch pattern that is to be worked over a multiple of 4 stitches in the sleeve. Therefore, I would round up to a total of 48 stitches, adding 4 stitches for each upper arm. Because there are two sleeves, this would mean an additional 8 total stitches in the neck circumference. The other option would be to work 2 additional shaping rows because, in basic raglan shaping, 2 stitches are added to each sleeve during each row. A third approach would be to divide the additional stitches in half, working one additional shaping row and adding the other 2 stitches to the neckline. None of these approaches is wrong or right, but the third option would probably most closely keep to the original design's proportions.

If you adjust the stitches in your upper arm, you will need to consider the impact on the stitches in the wrist/cuff. If you wish to keep the wrist the same size, you will need to work additional sleeve shaping rounds to account for the extra stitches. If you would like the wrist to be adjusted proportionally along with the added upper arm stitches, you can simply work the same number of shaping rounds, just note that your cuff will have those additional stitches in the end.

Wrist/Cuff

This measurement is more simple to adjust than the upper arm but the principles are the same. Use the Stitch Adjustment Worksheet, plugging in pattern information for the wrist. If the design is worked bottom-up, change the number of cast-on stitches to reflect your desired stitches. If the

pattern is worked top-down, work fewer decrease rounds to end at the appropriate number for your new wrist.

ADJUSTING LENGTH

In most cases, making length adjustments is even easier than adjusting the circumference. Adding or removing stitches takes more forethought than just knitting for shorter or longer distances. I do provide you with a Row Adjustment Worksheet for cases when shaping is involved. Using the worksheet will help you to determine where to add the length while preserving the intended shape.

Row Adjustment Worksheet — Length

A = ___ rows per 4 inches in gauge swatch
B = A/4 = ___ rows per 1 inch
     (do not round this number)
C = ___ desired length in inches
D = B x C = ___ desired number of total rows
E = ___ inches in pattern
F = B x E = ___ rows in pattern
G = D - F = ___ additional rows
H = ___ total shaping rows
I = ___ rows between shaping
J = G/H = ___ additional rows between shaping
K = I + J = ___ adjusted rows worked between shaping

Neck Depth

In this book, all the crewneck sweaters have lower front necklines than back necklines. To me, this is necessary shaping that makes the sweater more comfortable for its wearer and makes the garment look more polished. For this style of sweater on a boy, usually only a few inches do the trick. Too deep in the front and the sweater will look more like a scoop neck, which is not usually preferred for little lads. V-necks have more wiggle room in acceptable depth, and you might choose to adjust this measurement to go shallower or deeper depending on your personal preference. Just remember that if you do decide to make the neck depth shallower, you are simultaneously making the neck circumference smaller. Be sure your changes won't prevent the sweater from fitting over the recipient's head.

When you change the depth, you will need to consider the shaping rows, if they exist, and how they are affected. For a crewneck or circular neckline, work the shaping rows as directed on the area right above where the stitches are either placed on hold or cast on for the center front. Add the length and work the rows without neckline shaping at the top of the neck. For a V-neck, you'll want to work the Length Adjustment Worksheet all the way to the end to determine how many non-shaped rows you need to work in between shaping rows to still end up with a proportional V. If your change only results in a few extra rows, work them at the top of the neck as for a crewneck, but if you are changing the depth significantly, you will want to spread out these shaping rows as directed in the final calculation on the worksheet.

Neck depth is one of the trickier adjustments because there are two major components instead of just one—the number of center front stitches and the neckline shaping rows. When designed, these two numbers are calculated one based off of the other. This means that you have to also make sure they work together when you make your changes.

Sleeve Length

The final two sections are those which you should expect to modify most frequently, especially when trying to make a garment with Grow-with-Me flexibility. These adjustments are very much worth a few steps of math on the front end in order to potentially add years of life to your hand knit.

Oftentimes the very sign of "outgrown" is that sleeves are too short. Combine this with a long-limbed child and you are behind before you even bind off. If the boy you are knitting for has some extra-long arms, read this section closely and never make do with a designer's length suggestion again.

There are two major ways to add length to a sleeve. The first is to add length outside of the shaping, working without increasing or decreasing for however much longer you need your sleeve to be either before beginning your shaping or after completing it. This length should be added at the upper arm, not toward the wrist. If you are working a garment from the top down, this means your extra length would be worked before your first decrease round is worked, and conversely, for bottom-up sleeves you would complete all your increases and then work the extra length.

This is one downside to working top-down. One touted benefit to this construction method is that you can just "knit until it fits" after trying it on. Unfortunately, if you are simply following the sleeve instructions as written and then knitting extra length as needed at the end, it means that your decreases may be completed somewhere in the forearm area, which may result in an oddly snug bottom half of your sleeve. Just take a look at your own forearm right below your elbow and then closer to your wrist— there is a big difference in circumference between these two spots! Because you are much better off working this extra length at the top of the sleeve, you should instead know the length you want to add and work it prior to beginning those decreases. In most cases, adding this extra length at the top of the sleeve is totally legitimate and an easy way to accomplish your goal! The sleeve will still fit nicely. If you're a perfectionist and want to really match the original sleeve shape, read on.

The second way to add length to the sleeve is to maintain the shaping and spread the extra length throughout the sleeve. This will require our worksheet and a little math, but it will preserve the overall shape of the sleeve as the designer intended it.

Take a look at the example below. Note that E is the total number of inches on the schematic for sleeve length and C is the entry for the sleeve length that we want to end up with. The shaping rounds occur because our sleeve is narrower at the wrist than it is at the upper arm. Imagine that the shaping instruction for this sleeve is as follows: "Work Decrease Round a total of 7 times every 10 rounds." The entry for H is the total number of shaping rounds worked.

Row Adjustment Worksheet Example

A = 28 rows per 4 inches in gauge swatch
B = A/4 = 7 rows per 1 inch (do not round this number)
C = 15 desired length in inches
D = B x C = 105 desired number of total rows
E = 13 inches in pattern
F = B x E = 91 rows in pattern
G = D - F = 14 additional rows
H = 7 total shaping rows
I = 10 rows between shaping
J = G/H = 2 additional rows between shaping
K = I + J = 12 adjusted rows worked between shaping

After completing this worksheet we now have the key to our sleeve adjustment. The final computation K tells us that we need to work 12 rounds between each shaping row that the pattern originally called for. Our adjusted shaping instruction is as follows: "Work Decrease Round a total of 7 times every 12 rounds." Once completed, your sleeve should have the same length below and above the shaped portion of the sleeve as the pattern originally called for.

Garment Length

In boy's designs, adding total length to the garment is usually quite straightforward. In this book, none of the designs includes any kind of shaping at the waist, so the body is worked with the same number of stitches at the chest as are at the bottom. If you want to add length to the total length of the sweater, generally the best place to do it is in the body of the sweater, which describes the area from underarm to hem. If you are working a bottom-up design, add your length before joining the sleeves. If the design is constructed top-down, do it after you separate them. If you do decide to add length in the Yoke/Armhole Depth area, just make sure it is done outside of the shaping toward the underarm for the best-looking results. If you are working up a design outside of this book that does include body shaping, you can use the Row Adjustment Worksheet just like we did for the sleeve to determine how to keep that shaping intact.

Grow-with-Me Tips for Long-Lived-In Sweaters

You are now armed with all the necessary information to make pattern adjustments to fit your child's body precisely. You can add extra length where he grows the most, and you can adjust certain areas of the garment where you notice they are too snug. Now for the icing on the cake! Following are some of my favorite ways to create garments with extra life. These little tips can make the difference between one season of wear versus two to three. They aren't all suitable for every design, however. Some are worked into the sweater during the initial knit and others are add-ons later, but they require much less effort than knitting new sweaters every year. These tips can also save you if it's taken longer than planned to knit up a sweater, pushing back the date of delivery to the recipient.

Remember: kids grow up much more quickly than they grow out. Adding length rather than width is the golden rule of Grow-with-Me style. My goal is to provide you with options that look purposeful and polished, as opposed to

the common "he will grow into it" attitude that results in baggy sweaters that never seem to fit exactly right. Using these tips, you should have a good fit in multiple stages instead of just one either immediately or a few years later.

Tip #1

BUY EXTRA YARN AND SAVE YOUR SCRAPS

This might sound silly, but those scraps come in handy later on. When you finish a sweater project, put your leftover yarn in a clear plastic bag and label it with the name of the project and the needle size(s) you used to get gauge. If you don't have much left over, consider buying an extra skein if you think you might work some of the tips below that are completed once the sweater starts getting too small.

Tip #2

WORK TOP-DOWN

When possible, look for designs that are constructed from the top down. There are very good reasons for designs to be worked bottom-up, and tips for those projects are forthcoming, but if you're choosing between two similar sweaters and one is top-down, go with it. As the sweater starts to get short, borrow it back for the weekend (or the summer when it's not being worn). Get out your baggie with the scrap yarn from when you originally worked up the project (Tip #1!). Rip out the bound-off edges from the hems on the sleeves and body. Add the appropriate number of inches and bind off again. If there is a stitch pattern at the hem of your sweater, pull that out before adding your extra length and rework the hem when you're ready. With just a few hours of work, you have given new life to your project! Although I mentioned in the Sleeve Length section that I'm not a big fan of adding length to the bottom of a top-down sleeve, this is preferable to a sweater whose sleeves are too short.

Tip #3

THE ROLLED CUFF

A stockinette edge rolls. Some folks think this look is unfinished, but I happen to love it for boys because it makes the look a bit more casual. Depending on your fiber choice (more on this later), you can really adjust the length of knitting within the roll to suit a growing kiddo. You can roll up a couple of inches of length here. Then, as he grows, block it with pins and unroll length as needed. Work this roll on both the hem of the sleeves and the body, and you've banked some readymade growing room waiting to be let out.

Tip #4

THE ADDED CUFF

Did you work the Rolled Cuff but he still outgrew the length before outgrowing the chest size of the sweater? Of course, if you've worked the project top-down you can follow the steps in Tip #2. But one other option here is to add a ribbed (or other stitch pattern) cuff using the yarn you saved in Tip #1. You can either pick up and knit these edges with the new cuff options, or you can rip off a bound-off edge and resume knitting. Either way, with this tip you've not only added length and life but you've given the sweater a new look as well.

Tip #5

WORK A FOLDABLE HEM

Any type of ribbed sleeve cuff can be flipped upward and still look intentional. The stitch pattern doesn't even have to be a rib, it just has to be something that looks good from inside and out. Make your sleeve overlong and have him flip that cuff as long as he needs to.

Tip #6

USE A TURNING RIDGE

This trick is worked up when the sweater is first knit, and the hems that are created can be let out later on. It works on both top-down and bottom-up projects and gives the sweater two different finished looks. A turning ridge is a right side row that is purled or a wrong side row that is knit (both result in the same look on the right side of the work). If the design contains a hem that is different than the stitch pattern in the body (for example, the body is worked in stockinette and the hem is ribbed), add this turning ridge row in between the hem and body. Repeat for cuff and sleeve. If the design does not have a different stitch pattern for hem and body, you'll need to choose one for the hem. The most simple is a 1x1 rib, but it really does not matter what you choose—pretty much anything except for stockinette will work. Keep the number of stitches on your needle in mind when choosing this stitch pattern—you won't want to have to manipulate the stitch count significantly to work this new hem. Remember that whatever your hem stitch pattern is, the length in this hem should be additional to what the pattern suggests for the length in the body. If you're working bottom-up, measure from the turning ridge before working your sleeve join instead of from the cast-on edge. If you are working top-down, work your turning ridge at the finished length of the sweater and not prior. Once the sweater is knit, use a tapestry needle and a length of yarn to stitch the hem and cuffs in place toward the wrong side of the sweater. When you need the extra length, remove the seam and block the hems out. You can make your hems up to 2 inches long and still have them look natural and intentional.

Tip #7

ADD EXTRA LENGTH FROM THE GET-GO

This one might seem a bit obvious, but it's still worth mentioning. It's easier to get away with this in the body of the sweater than it is in the sleeves, but if you do it in conjunction with Tip #5, it's a very classic way to add growing room. There is a wide variety in acceptable lengths for sweaters. Avoid a sweater that is so long that it falls within 1 inch of the crotch. But there is a 2- to 3-inch sweet spot where sweaters can hit and look great. If you are able to measure your recipient and work to the longest point initially, in the following year it will hit him a little higher but still work.

Tip #8

USE A STRETCHY STITCH PATTERN

A couple of the projects in this book use this tip! When you use a rib (Library Cardigan) or waffle stitch (Long John PJs) or anything stretchy, you'll get some extra help opening up that chest size. Waffle style stitch patterns stretch vertically as well as horizontally, so they can give you some wiggle room in length, too.

Tip #9

RIP IT OUT

The final suggestion I have for you might sound a little scary if you've never done it before. However, it is well worth the trouble and if you follow these directions, it is not risky at all. You'll need to have followed Tip #1 and have some project yarn left to work with. Place a lifeline into the bottom of the sweater a row or two above the hem. If your project was worked top-down, you can conserve some yarn by ripping out your hem all the way to the lifeline, instead of cutting. But if you worked bottom-up, you'll want to go ahead and make a cut through your sweater several rows below the lifeline, then just take out those few rows left until your lifeline holds your live stitches at the ready. Place the live stitches on your needles, and start knitting. For top-down projects, you should be able to seamlessly work in pattern exactly as you had before for the desired length, then rework the hem, bind off, and repeat this process for the sleeves. For bottom-up projects, options are limited by stitch pattern. If the body is worked in stockinette, you can go ahead and add length as for top-down projects. However if the stitch pattern in the body is textural, with knits and purls or cables, you will not be able to add rows in the body because your work will be off by half a stitch. Instead, you will want to begin a new hem and you'll add your length into this section instead. Repeat for the sleeves.

Stylistic Customizations and Additions

Sizing is not the only way you may wish to customize your knits. There are all sorts of tweaks you make to perfect a project for its recipient. When making substantive pattern changes, always think about how your changes will affect the way a garment fits before getting underway. Planning ahead for these changes is crucial for making them successful modifications.

Changing Stitch Patterns

Perhaps you love the construction and style of a garment but prefer to work it in a different stitch pattern than is called for. This is a great way to insert your own style into a piece, but make sure to think through your adjustment before beginning, particularly with regard to the stitch repeat.

STITCH REPEAT

If a piece is being worked in the round, you will need to make sure that the stitch repeat of the pattern fits evenly into the number of stitches within the garment. If it does not fit, you will need to modify the stitch pattern itself or the number of stitches in the garment. For example, all of the colorwork options for the Imagination sweater are worked over a multiple of 4 stitches. Suppose you wanted to use a stitch pattern you have seen elsewhere that is based on an 8-stitch repeat and you are working the size 10. This size is worked over 156 stitches total in the chest (where colorwork is performed). 156 cannot be divided evenly by 8. Therefore, to make this pattern work, it would need to be adjusted to another multiple. 156 is divisible by 6. So, perhaps you might choose to go with another pattern worked over 6 stitches. Or, you could increase by 4 stitches in the chest of the sweater in order to get to 160, which is indeed divisible by 8. If instead you were working the size 6 of this same pattern, there are 136 chest stitches total and this number does evenly divide by 8. This time your substitute stitch pattern could be used without adjustment. If all this sounds too complicated for you, remember only this: substitute stitch patterns that divide evenly into your project stitch count.

If a piece is being worked flat, back and forth, it is a little easier to make substitutions because it is not necessarily important for exact repeats to be completed. Instead there can be partial repeats on the edges of the knit. Substitute at will, just remember how many extra stitches there are on the edge so that your pattern does not shift back and forth.

TEXTURE AND GAUGE

Going from a stockinette stitch pattern to any textural stitch pattern usually affects your gauge. This is why it is always important to swatch using your stitch pattern. In cabling, the act of twisting stitches will tighten up a knitter's gauge to some extent. This tightening makes cabled borders appealing for items with negative ease, as the extra snugness helps to hold the item in place. If you intend to use a cable as a main feature of a design, make sure to use the cable repeat in your gauge swatch. You might find that you need to use a heavier weight yarn and larger needles to match the gauge of the original piece if it was worked in a stockinette stitch pattern.

Using knits and purls together may have the opposite effect on your gauge. Instead of stitches becoming smaller and closer together as when using cables, a knitter's tension may be looser as their yarn is moved from back to front or vice versa. This is why many patterns suggest using a smaller needle for a ribbed hem than for the main component of the design. As with a cabled stitch pattern, make sure to swatch in your texture pattern if you intend to use it as a main feature of the project. You might need to drop down a needle size or two.

ADDING COLOR

Stranded colorwork describes a style of knitting where unused colors are gently carried on the wrong side of the work. Most of these projects are also worked in stockinette, so you might be tempted to assume that your gauge when working with one color in stockinette will be the same as when working two or more in stranded stockinette. Because the strands in the back create an extra layer of fabric, this may or may not be true. Again, always use the stitch pattern you intend to use in your garment when working up your gauge swatch. It takes practice to carry the yarn at an even level of tension, and if you pull it too tightly, your gauge will become even smaller. Additionally, the extra layer of yarn in the back makes the fabric less elastic, so there is less wiggle room for gauge differences. If you want to add color to an otherwise stockinette design, the easiest way to do so without having to worry about gauge is by using stripes. Horizontal stripes can be worked over any multiple of stitches because there is only one color used in each row—they should not have an impact on your gauge.

ROWS OR ROUNDS

I mentioned in the Gauge section that working back and forth can produce a different gauge than working in the round. Aside from gauge there is another consideration related to construction for the introduction of stitch patterns to a design. If a stitch pattern is repeated on an odd number of rounds, it may not be an appropriate pattern for a design that has any component worked back and forth. Remember, lots of sweaters that are primarily worked in the round still have work that is completed back and forth, primarily in the yoke. Usually, the neckline shaping needs to be worked back and forth.

If your neckline shaping is only worked over a few rows (a crewneck for example), you can discontinue your stitch pattern at that point and complete the project in stockinette, or you can usually fudge the pattern enough to make it work for such a small area. But, if you are working something with a deep placket or V-neck, you could run into trouble. In a cabled project, if the cabled round is performed every 3 rounds, you'll be stuck attempting to cable on a wrong side row for every other repeat. In a stranded colorwork project, if one color is *not* used for an even number of rounds at a time, it will be left at the end of a row and not available to you when you need it again at the beginning of that row, resulting in a lot of cut yarn and ends to weave in—again, doable when you're talking about a few rows at the top of the neckline but perhaps not so much for 6 inches of knitting. I am guilty of starting a project in the round and working on it for way too many inches before having the realization that I would be in trouble after a back-and-forth switch in the yoke! Don't let this happen to you. Plan ahead.

Doable Add-Ons: Pockets and Hoods

POCKETS

There are two things that make my boys incredibly invested in what I am knitting for them. The first is finding out it will have a zipper (much easier to open and close than buttons). The second is learning that it has pockets! My kids are collectors. The downside is that I have to check for rocks and lizards and crayons in these pockets on a regular basis, but it is well worth it knowing that they have a safe little place to store these "treasures." One of my first children's sweater designs was the Treasure Vest, which features a kangaroo pocket on the front (just like the Cooper Hoodie). The idea came from my oldest son's "treasure walks"—walks during which I would grit my teeth and

allow him to pick up and save all sorts of things he would find in the woods. Allow me to make your knitting equally impressive. I'll show you the ropes to adding several different types of pockets to any sweater that you want.

Horizontal Set-In Pocket

This pocket is worked into the sweater while it's being knit. For a bottom-up project, its lining is knit separately and then worked into a row on the sweater body. In a top-down design, the lining is worked over a small area with stitches for the front of the pocket cast-on over them. For both methods, the knit lining remains on the wrong side of the fabric and is eventually sewn on with scrap yarn and a tapestry needle around the bottom edge and two sides. Follow the steps below to add this type of pocket onto any sweater constructed vertically.

1. Use the Stitch Adjustment Worksheet, lines A to D, to determine how many stitches wide your pocket will be. You can determine your desired width by measuring a pocket on an existing item or you can use one of the projects in this book as an example (Library Cardigan, for example, has pockets though they are not set-in). If you are working a bottom-up project, knit your lining(s), back and forth, with the desired number of stitches to your desired depth. Leave the stitches on a spare DPN and break yarn.

2. Decide where you would like to place your pockets. Most set-in pockets are on either side of the front or in the underarm area. They are usually in places where his hands would naturally rest, so you don't want them to be too high up on the body. You could also create a breast pocket, or even a fancy pocket on the sleeve. It is totally up to you where you will put your pocket. You will need to know where the *top* of the pocket will be in order to inset the lining properly.

3. Decide what you would like the top of the pocket to look like. This will determine what you do with the stitches on the body that fall where the lining will be placed. If you are working bottom-up, you will eventually bind off these stitches, but you may first choose to work a few rows of ribbing or another stitch pattern to decorate them; do this before proceeding to the next step. If you are working a pattern top-down, you will be casting on stitches and you'll need to know what to do with them right off the bat. Proceed to step 4a for bottom-up design, 4b for top-down.

4a. Joining Row (bottom-up design): Work to pocket placement, slip onto a stitch holder the same number of stitches as are on your pocket lining or bind off these stitches (shown). With working yarn, knit across pocket lining, with right side of lining facing. Resume knitting on the body and work to the end of row (or, to your second pocket and repeat the joining instructions).

4b. Separating Row (top-down design): Work to pocket placement, slip the same number of stitches to hold as you would like on your pocket lining. With working yarn, cast on the same number of stitches as you slipped to hold. Resume knitting on the body and work to the end of row (or, to your second pocket and repeat the separating instructions). Work your pocket lining to the desired depth during finishing. Don't forget to work the top of your pocket as desired over the next few rows.

continued

5. Continue working your pattern as instructed. During finishing, use scrap yarn and a tapestry needle to sew the pocket lining to the wrong side of your project.

Kangaroo Pocket

This style of pocket is featured on the Cooper Hoodie. It is set in the center of the garment and the top of the pocket is generally narrower than the bottom. For this pocket, the pocket front is knit separately, and then seamlessly attached to the sweater while being knit. Alternatively, you can sew the pocket on afterwards. Follow the steps below to add this type of pocket onto any sweater constructed vertically. I've broken up these instructions into two parts: first, working up the pocket, and second, attaching it to the sweater.

Make the Pocket

1. Use the Stitch Adjustment Worksheet, lines A to D, to determine how many stitches wide your pocket will be at the bottom. You can determine your desired width by measuring a pocket on an existing item or using one of the projects in this book as an example (Cooper Hoodie, for example). Next, determine how wide you want the pocket to be on the top. In order to center the pocket properly, look at the number of stitches on the front of your sweater—if it is an even number of stitches, the number of stitches on your pocket should also be even, if it is an odd number, make your total number of pocket stitches odd. Likewise, if the number of stitches on the bottom of the pocket is odd, the top needs to be as well, and the same goes if it is even.

2. Determine how many total Decrease Rows you will need to work. Subtract the number of stitches for the top of your pocket from the number of stitches on the bottom. Divide this number by 2. This is your total number of Decrease Rows.

3. Determine how often you will work the Decrease Row as follows. First, use the Row Adjustment Worksheet, lines A to D, to determine how many total rows will be in your pocket. Then, divide the total number of rows in your pocket by the number of Decrease Rows you calculated in step 2. The resulting number will tell you how often you will be working a Decrease Row. You will want to round this number to the closest even number. So, if it is 4.75, round to 4. If it is 5.25, you might want to round up to 6. This will allow you to always be working a Decrease Row on a right side row.

4. Construct the pocket as follows:
    Provisionally cast on stitches for the bottom of your pocket.
    Work at least 2 rows before your first Decrease Row.
    Decrease Row: K1, ssk, work to last 3 sts, k2tog, k1.
    Work Decrease Row as calculated in step 3.
    Leave the stitches on a spare DPN and break yarn.

Attach the Pocket

Seamlessly attaching the pocket to the sweater requires you to do a little unorthodox stitch manipulation, but the result is polished and perfectly centered. Follow the relevant set of directions below (one describes the procedure when working top-down and the other bottom-up). Instructions begin on the round where you are ready to perform the first join—for top-down this is the top of the pocket to the sweater and for bottom-up, it is the bottom of the pocket to the sweater.

Seamless Attachment to a Top-Down Project

1. Using safety pins or removable stitch markers, mark the placement of the top of the pocket on your working needles. To do this, first mark the center front of your sweater using your knowledge of where the end-of-round marker is located. If there is an even number of stitches on the front, put your first marker in between those two stitches. If there is an odd number of stitches, place one marker on either side of the center stitch. Then, count an equal number of stitches away from the center markers on either side and place additional markers where the pocket begins and ends. For pockets with an even number of stitches, this number is simply the total number of top pocket stitches divided by two. For odd stitch count pockets, subtract 1 (the center stitch) from the stitch count before dividing in half. Do *not* remove the center marker(s) even after joining pocket top.

2. Work in pattern to the first pocket marker, remove marker. Hold pocket upside down so that right side of pocket is against right side of sweater, and wrong side of pocket is facing you. Knit 1 stitch from DPN together with 1 stitch from circular needle and continue in this manner until all stitches from top of pocket are joined; remove second marker.

3. Work even until length matches pocket from top of join. Remove provisional cast-on from bottom of pocket and place stitches on spare DPN, ready to work right side.

4. Place markers for bottom of pocket on your needles just like you did in step 1, only this time use the number of stitches that are on the bottom of the pocket instead of on the top, using the center marker(s) that should still be in place.

continued

5. Work in pattern to first pocket marker, remove marker. Flip pocket upward so that wrong side of pocket is against right side of sweater. Join stitches as for top of pocket; remove remaining pocket markers.

Seamless Attachment to a Bottom-Up Project

1. Using safety pins or removable stitch markers, mark the placement of the bottom of the pocket on your working needles. To do this, first mark the center front of your sweater using your knowledge of where the end-of-round marker is located. If there is an even number of stitches on the front, put your first marker in between those two stitches. If there is an odd number of stitches, place one marker on either side of the center stitch. Then, count an equal number of stitches away from the center marker(s) on either side and place additional markers where the pocket begins and ends. For pockets with an even number of stitches, this number is simply the total number of bottom pocket stitches divided by two. For odd stitch count pockets, subtract 1 (the center stitch) from the stitch count before dividing in half. Do *not* remove the center marker(s) even after joining pocket bottom.

2. Remove provisional cast-on from bottom of pocket and place stitches on spare DPN, ready to work right side. Work in pattern to the first pocket marker; remove marker. Hold pocket upside down so that right side of pocket is against right side of sweater. Knit 1 stitch from DPN together with 1 stitch from circular needle and continue in this manner

until all stitches from bottom of pocket are joined. You can reference the photos at left for the bottom-up project, just note that the pocket will appear upside down in those photos.

3. Work even until length matches pocket from bottom of join.

4. Place markers for top of pocket on your needles just like you did in step 1, only this time use the number of stitches that are on the top of the pocket instead of on the bottom, using the center marker(s) that should still be in place.

5. Work in pattern to first pocket marker; remove marker. Flip pocket upward so that wrong side of pocket is against right side of sweater. Join stitches as for bottom of pocket; remove remaining pocket markers.

The only finishing required for this method of pocket attachment is to tighten up the corners of the pocket if necessary. You can also choose to add ribbing or other type of edging to the sides of the pocket in which case the top and the bottom of the edging will also need to be tacked down to the sweater.

Vertical Set-In Pocket

This pocket is featured in the Jake Jacket. These pockets typically hit on the front toward each side and are perfect complements to jacket-style garments, among others. The linings for these pockets are worked separately and attached to the wrong side of the sweater, and the openings for the pockets are created by working the body in separate sections for the entire depth of the pocket. Follow the steps below to add this type of pocket onto any sweater constructed vertically.

1. Determine the depth of your pockets. If you are working top-down, you will need to know the length your sweater should be when you need to begin working short rows at the top of the pocket. For bottom-up projects, know where you want the bottom of the pocket to begin.

2. Determine the placement of your pocket(s). If you are working two pockets, you will want to make sure they are located at the same place on either side of the body.

3. Work in pattern until you arrive at the decided length to separate the body for the pocket opening(s), ending after a wrong side row. Place marker(s) for the pocket. Work to marker, turn your piece (do not wrap), and work back and forth over this section of stitches only to the finished depth of the pocket, ending after a right side row; break yarn. Your working needle should be ready to move on to the next section.

4. Attach yarn again at the bottom of the pocket. Begin knitting and work this next section just as you did the first. If you are working a second pocket on the other side of the sweater, make sure you turn and work back and forth as marked. Repeat for the next section if applicable. Once all sections are an even length, you should be ready to work a wrong side row.

5. During the next row, work across the entire piece, joining all sections back together. You have created the opening(s) for your pocket(s). Work the rest of the pattern as directed.

6. Use the Stitch Adjustment Worksheet, lines A to D, to determine how many stitches need to be in your pocket lining. Multiply your pocket depth by 2 and use this as the circumference of your lining. Work your lining as follows: With a DPN, cast on your total number of stitches. With two DPNs, slip first stitch to one DPN and second stitch to second DPN. Continue so that alternating sts are on two DPNs. Place marker and join to work in the round. Knit in the round until lining is as deep as desired. This lining will hang from your sweater toward the center front, so make sure it is not so long that it appears in a buttonband area or falls below the hem. Bind off all stitches, leaving a long tail for sewing.

continued

7. Pocket Finishing: Your pocket will look better if you work an edging on the front side of the lining. This will be the side of the opening that is closest to center front. Pick up and knit stitches and work your edging as desired. Use the yarn tails to stitch the top and bottom sides of the edging to the sweater. Lastly, sew the bound-off edge of the pocket lining all the way around the pocket opening on the wrong side of the sweater.

Patch Pocket

The last pocket I'll present may technically be the easiest, but has the greatest probability of appearing off-kilter if not executed properly. This is because it is seamed and not worked into the garment. A patch pocket is simply that: a pocket based on one little piece of fabric that is then patched onto the garment. You can work this pocket in any shape (many kangaroo pockets are worked this way, actually) and place it anywhere on the garment. One alternative to knitting the pocket separately from the garment is to pick up and knit stitches for the bottom of the pocket from the finished sweater and then seam the sides of the pocket after it is completed. Feel free to use this method by making that one simple change in step 1 below. The instructions begin after your sweater is already completed. Follow the steps below to add this type of pocket onto any sweater.

1. Use the Stitch Adjustment Worksheet, lines A to D, to determine how many stitches wide your pocket will be. You can determine your desired width by measuring a pocket on an existing item or using one of the projects in this book as an example (Library Cardigan has patch pockets). Decide if you want the top or side(s) of your pocket to feature any edging. Knit your pocket back and forth as desired and bind off all stitches.

2. Use scrap yarn in a contrasting color and a tapestry needle to outline the pocket placement on your sweater. Weave the yarn through a single column, across a row, up the column on the other side, and back across to the point where you began. This outline will help you to seam the pocket in exactly the right spot. If you are doing two pockets, you will want to count rows and stitches to make sure that your pockets are in exactly the same spot on either side. It is amazing how obvious one stitch or row off can be.

3. Using the outline as a guide, stitch your pocket onto the sweater. Remember not to seam the opening of the pocket to the sweater!

The trick to this pocket is utilizing the contrasting yarn outline and good seaming skills. If seaming isn't your specialty just yet, practice with some old gauge swatches before attaching your pocket to your sweater. And remember, you can always rip out a seam and try it again.

HOODS

Your first time making a hood may catch you off guard—you think once you start to knit the hood that you are almost finished with your project, and then you realize that it is really quite a large chunk of knitting! This is especially true for knits for kids since their heads are larger in proportion to their bodies compared to adults. Your hood will probably be somewhere in the neighborhood of fifteen to twenty percent of the entire project.

There are many different ways to successfully shape a hood, but here, I'll go over one basic method that works consistently and is simple to execute. You can experiment with different types of neckline shaping as well, but I'll detail one straightforward mini V style here. As with most sweaters, you want somewhat of a dip in the front so that the chin isn't irritated by the bottom of the hood (collar). This simple mini V-neck is a great option.

The instructions below are written for pullovers. Hoods can be added even more easily to cardigans. Because cardigans are usually already set up for button bands or zipper bands, you should not need to perform any additional neckline shaping for a hood. You can skip right on ahead to the Hood Math section. The one style of cardigan that's really not well suited for a hood is a shawl collar neckline, so I do not recommend using these instructions for that particular style.

Neckline Math

The following example instructions are based on a worsted weight project with a Neck Depth of 10 rows, which should be approximately 1.5 inches, and a hood edging width of 1 inch. If you are working a project at another gauge, you can use the Stitch and Row Adjustment Worksheets, lines A to D, to determine how many rows back you should work the Neckline Shaping Row and how many stitches wide to make your edging. Choose the appropriate section to get your neckline set up based on the construction of your project. Either way, you're going to be tossing the neckline shaping instructions in your existing pattern out the window and replacing them with these. Note that you will still need to work any sweater body shaping (such as raglan or other style yoke shaping) that occurs at the same time.

Bottom-Up

Continue working in the round until there are 10 rows left before the top of your sweater. If your pattern is set up with a lower neckline, work any yoke/raglan shaping in the round instead of back and forth as your pattern might direct. If the front of your sweater has an even number of stitches, your center front will consist of 4 stitches; if it has an odd number of stitches, use 5 stitches for the center front instead.

Neckline Shaping Row: Work to center front stitches, bind off these 4 or 5 stitches; starting at right front, work

Hood Sizing Chart

Size	4	6	8	10	12
Hood Height (in.)	12	12	12.5	12.5	13
(cm)	30.5	30.5	31.75	31.75	33
Hood Width (in.)	19.75	20.25	20.75	21.25	21.5
(cm)	50	51.5	53	54	54.5

the final 9–10 rows (depending on the location of your end of round marker) as the pattern directs, making sure to complete all body shaping. If your pattern is not worked in stockinette, work the first and last stitches of every row in stockinette to make it easier to pick up stitches for the hood edging later.

The total number of stitches left on your needles will form the beginning of your hood. Take note of this number.

Top-Down

Before beginning your project, examine your cast-on instructions and determine how many stitches are in the back neck portion and the front(s). In many cases, there will be only 1 or 2 stitches cast on for each front. Add the number of stitches for each front together and subtract these stitches from the back neck stitches. If the total number of back neck stitches is odd, subtract another 5 stitches from this total. If it is even, subtract 4 stitches instead. The number you are left with is the total of additional stitches that need to be cast on to modify the neckline for the hood. The 4 or 5 center front stitches will be left open until they are added in during the Neckline Shaping Row. So, add the total additional stitches to your pattern's original cast on number, and provisionally cast on this total number of stitches. Now, divide the number of total additional stitches in half. This is the number of stitches added to each front. During the following round, make sure you note these additional stitches as you are setting up for the yoke/raglan shaping that your pattern directs.

To make this more concrete, here's an example. The following lines are the first from the Striated Crew. For simplicity, I have removed all numbers except those from the smallest size.

Original Instructions

With circular needles, crochet hook, and scrap yarn, provisionally CO 35 sts.

Row 1 (WS): P1, pm, p1, pm, p4, pm, p1, pm, p21, pm, p1, pm, p4, pm, p1, pm, p1.

Neckline Math

Original Back Neck stitches: 21 (an odd number)
Original Front Stitches: 1 on each side

21 (Back Neck) − 1 (Front 1) − 1 (Front 2) − 5 (center front) = 14
New Cast-On Number: 35 + 14 = 49
Additional Front Stitches: 14/2 = 7
New Total for Each Front : 7 + 1 = 8

Modified Neckline Instructions

With circular needles, crochet hook, and scrap yarn, provisionally CO 49 sts.

Row 1 (WS): P8, pm, p1, pm, p4, pm, p1, pm, p21, pm, p1, pm, p4, pm, p1, pm, p8.

The total number of cast-on stitches will form the beginning of your hood. If your pattern is not worked in stockinette, work the first and last stitches of every row in stockinette to make it easier to pick up stitches for the hood edging later. After determining your cast-on adjustment and your changes to the set-up row, work 9 or 10 rows according to the pattern, ending after a right side row and disregarding any existing neckline shaping. *Do not turn.*

Neckline Shaping Row: Cable cast-on center front stitches, join to work in the round.

Continue working the project according to the pattern; your front should now have the same number of stitches each round as does your back. Place your end-of-round marker according to where your pattern instructs.

Hood Math

Recall the total number of stitches on your neckline. For the bottom-up sweater, this was the number left after the center front stitches were bound off and the body shaping was completed. For the top-down sweater, this was the number of stitches that were provisionally cast on. Note whether this total number of stitches is odd or even.

Use the Hood Sizing Chart to determine the hood height and width desired. If you know you'd like to make a larger or smaller hood, you can use your own measurements. Our neckline set-up was created to suit a 1-inch hood edging. Because the edging will be on both sides of the hood, subtract 2 inches from the desired total hood width. Next, use the Stitch Adjustment Worksheet to determine how many stitches you will want to have at the widest part of your hood, based on the last calculation.

Basic Hood Pattern

With neckline sts on the needle, ready to work the RS, work as follows.

Increase Row (RS): K1, M1L, work to last st, M1R, k1.

Work Increase Row every RS row a total of X times.

Work back and forth in pattern until hood reaches the desired height.

Split hood stitches in half and fold inward so that the hood RS are together and work a three-needle bind-off. If the total number of hood stitches is odd, work an extra stitch last and bind it off as well.

Finishing: Starting at right front neckline, pick up and knit 3 sts for every 4 rows all the way around hood, ending with an odd number of sts.

Next Row (WS): *P1, k1; rep from * to last st, p1.

Work in 1x1 rib for one inch; bind off all sts.

Use yarn tails or scraps to stitch side of edging to center front neckline, placing the right front edging underneath the left front edging (if you're knitting for a little lady, you can reverse this and place right front edging on top).

Round up to the nearest odd or even number that matches the number of neckline stitches in your project.

Determine how many total Increase Rows you will need to work. Subtract the number of stitches on your neckline from the total number of stitches at the top. Divide this number by 2. This is your total number of Increase Rows, call it X for the pattern below.

You are now ready to knit the hood! If your project has a stitch pattern, you can feel free to continue it in the hood. The suggested increases here are worked one stitch in at the edge and you can adjust them to your pattern on the following row if desired. I do suggest that you work the outside stitches in stockinette on every row, as it will be easier to pick up stitches for your edging. If your neckline stitches were provisionally cast on, go ahead and remove that cast on and place the stitches on your needles.

Materials, Techniques, and Abbreviations

Yarn Matters

I have chosen some of my favorite yarns for the projects in this book. There is a huge variety among them, and if you're fortunate enough to find them conveniently and be able to use them in your knitting, you won't have to give this particular section much attention. But if you're planning on substituting yarn, please do read on. There are two major components to yarn choice for a knitting project: weight and fiber content.

The yarn weights used in this book range from fingering to bulky. Fingering is the finest used, followed by sport, double knitting or DK, worsted, aran, and bulky. Weight of the yarn is particularly pertinent with regard to gauge. Technically, you can "get gauge" with many different weights of yarn by adjusting your needle size. However, a lighter weight yarn with a larger needle will result in a looser fabric and a heavier weight yarn with a smaller needle will result

in a tighter fabric. This is the background to the needle recommendations you see on the back of yarn labels.

Some designs intentionally use an unexpected needle size for interesting fabric. The looser a fabric, the more drape it tends to have. A tighter fabric is preferable for a stuffed toy because it prevents stuffing from coming out through the stitches. For the most part, the projects in this book are worked within recommended needle size. Therefore, if you intend to substitute yarn, you will want to try and match the weight of the yarn suggested in the pattern as closely as possible for the best results.

Fiber content describes the makeup of the yarn. Yarn can be made up of animal fibers, plant fibers, and/or man-made fibers. Animal fibers such as wool and alpaca generally provide the most warmth. These fibers are also feltable, unless they are superwash. They are preferred in stranded colorwork projects because, over time, both the stitches in the project and the strands on the wrong side of the work will actually felt together and blend the colorwork naturally. Superwash yarns have been through a process that prevents the wool from felting by either adding a coat to each strand or stripping the strands of the scales that would have otherwise meshed together. These yarns can be a great option for most projects, although for colorwork I still prefer feltable yarns. Animal fibers also have good "memory," which means that if you work with them during blocking (e.g., rolling or unrolling a stockinette hem; see page 13), you can convince them to do what you want.

Plant fibers such as bamboo and cotton are less stretchy and have more drape than wool. They result in cooler fabrics, which are nice for some climates (like where I live in sunny South Carolina). Fabrics made with these fibers can grow much larger when blocked, so take special care to block your gauge swatch fully before taking your measurements.

Acrylics and other man-made fibers can be nice and stretchy, but they do not provide the same warmth as animal fibers. They also do not have the same type of memory. I don't recommend acrylics for my Grow-with-Me rolled stockinette hem trick because it's almost impossible to straighten out these hems in acrylic. However, man-made fibers can be a great alternative if machine washability is important to you.

Be sure to look at and follow the washing instructions of whatever yarn you choose. Many prefer to use only washable yarns for their children's projects. There is value to

knowing that an accidental toss in the washing machine isn't going to ruin all that work. However, I do not recommend regularly throwing any hand knits in your washing machine unless you are using a delicate wool cycle. While certain yarns might be machine-safe, without felting properties they run a real risk of ends coming undone and projects unraveling in the machine, which can ruin a project just as quickly as a serious shrink. Because I don't use regular machine cycles anyway, "machine wash" is not a requirement for me when choosing yarn even for a rough and tumble boy's sweater.

Techniques

Cable Cast-On

In this book, this cast-on is the recommended method for adding stitches in the middle of a row. You will work the cast-on into an existing stitch on your needle. *Insert the RH needle into the space between the last 2 sts on the LH needle, wrap your yarn around needle as if to knit and pull the new stitch through. Transfer the stitch to your LH needle. Repeat from * for desired number of stitches.

Crochet Chain

Make a slip knot and slide it onto crochet hook. *Holding the yarn in your left hand, grab yarn with hook from front

Standard Yarn Weight System

Categories of yarn, gauge ranges, and recommended needle and hook sizes

Yarn Weight Symbol & Category Names	0 LACE	1 SUPER FINE	2 FINE	3 LIGHT	4 MEDIUM	5 BULKY	6 SUPER BULKY
Type of Yarns in Category	Fingering 10-count crochet thread	Sock, Fingering, Baby	Sport, Baby	DK, Light Worsted	Worsted, Afghan, Aran	Chunky, Craft, Rug	Bulky, Roving
Knit Gauge Range* in Stockinette Stitch to 4 inches	33–40** sts	27–32 sts	23–26 sts	21–24 st	16–20 sts	12–15 sts	6–11 sts
Recommended Needle in Metric Size Range	1.5–2.25 mm	2.25–3.25 mm	3.25–3.75 mm	3.75–4.5 mm	4.5–5.5 mm	5.5–8 mm	8 mm and larger
Recommended Needle U.S. Size Range	000–1	1 to 3	3 to 5	5 to 7	7 to 9	9 to 11	11 and larger
Crochet Gauge* Ranges in Single Crochet to 4 inches	32–42 double crochets**	21–32 sts	16–20 sts	12–17 sts	11–14 sts	8–11 sts	5–9 sts
Recommended Hook in Metric Size Range	Steel*** 1.6–1.4 mm	2.25–3.5 mm	3.5–4.5 mm	4.5–5.5 mm	5.5–6.5 mm	6.5–9 mm	9 mm and larger
Recommended Hook U.S. Size Range	Steel*** 6, 7, 8 Regular hook B–1	B–1 to E–4	E–4 to 7	7 to I–9	I–9 to K–10 1/2	K–10 1/2 to M–13	M–13 and larger

  * GUIDELINES ONLY: The above reflect the most commonly used gauges and needle or hook sizes for specific yarn categories.
 ** Lace weight yarns are usually knitted or crocheted on larger needles and hooks to create lacy, openwork patterns. Accordingly, a gauge range is difficult to determine. Always follow the gauge stated in your pattern.
*** Steel crochet hooks are sized differently from regular hooks—the higher the number, the smaller the hook, which is the reverse of regular hook sizing.

This Standards & Guidelines booklet and downloadable symbol artwork are available at: YarnStandards.com

to back, and draw hook with yarn back through previous stitch on hook to form a new stitch. Repeat from * to desired length.

I-Cord

Use two DPNs to work I-cord.

1. Knit across sts on LH needle, do not turn.

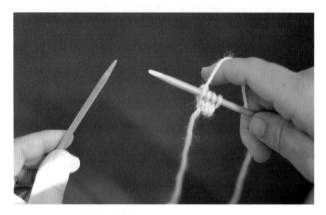

2. Slide sts to other end of DPN.

3. Pull working yarn behind work tightly and use it to knit the next row. The more tightly you can pull the yarn when starting a new row, the more even your cord will be.

Repeat steps 1–3 to desired length.

I-Cord Bind-Off

Use a spare DPN with your working LH needle to perform this bind-off. Cable CO 3 sts onto LH needle. *K2, k2tog tbl, sl the three sts on RH needle back to LH needle. Repeat from * until only 3 sts remain. BO 3 sts.

Jeny's Surprisingly Stretchy Bind-Off

Each stitch will be processed with a yarn over prior to being bound off. *To process a knit stitch:* YFON, k1, sl yo over knit st. *To process a purl st:* Yo, p1, sl yo over purl st. *To bind off:* Process the first two stitches, pass right stitch over left and off needle, [process next stitch, pass right stitch over left and off needle] until 1 st rem. Cut yarn, weave through rem st and secure.

Kitchener Stitch

Place two sets of live stitches on needles. Hold needles so that they are parallel to each other and are both held in LH with tips facing the same direction and WS of the fabric together. Thread yarn into tapestry needle and set up as follows: Insert the needle in the first stitch on the front needle as if to purl, leaving the stitch on the needle and pulling yarn through, insert the needle in the first stitch on the back needle as if to knit, leaving the stitch on the needle and pulling yarn through. The following four steps will be repeated until all stitches are grafted.

1. Insert the needle in the first stitch on the front needle as if to knit, slipping the stitch off the needle.

2. Insert the needle into the next stitch on the front needle as if to purl, leaving the stitch on the needle and pulling the yarn through.

3. Insert the needle into the first stitch on the back needle as if to purl, slipping the stitch off the needle.

4. Insert the needle into the next stitch on the back needle as if to knit, leaving the stitch on the needle.

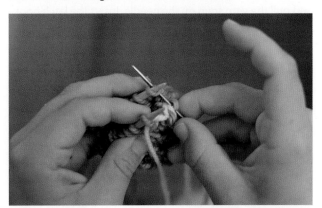

When there is only one stitch remaining on each needle, work step 1 immediately followed by step 3. Break yarn. Use tapestry needle to snug up any stitches so that the gauge matches that of the project.

One-Row Buttonhole

Starting at buttonhole, WYIF, sl 1 st. Move yarn to back. *Sl 1 st, pass first sl st over second and off needle; repeat from * to BO desired number of sts. Sl last st on RH needle back to LH needle. Turn. Cable CO the number of sts that were BO. CO one additional st, but before transferring new st to LH needle, bring yarn to front between new st and first st on LH needle. Turn. Sl 1 st, pass first st over second and off needle to close buttonhole.

Provisional Cast-On

Make a slip knot with scrap yarn and slide it onto crochet hook. Hold your crochet hook perpendicular to your working needle, with crochet hook closer to you.

1. Wrap yarn around back of working needle and from left to right in front of crochet hook.

continued

2. Draw crochet hook down to catch the loop of yarn and pull it through loop on crochet hook.

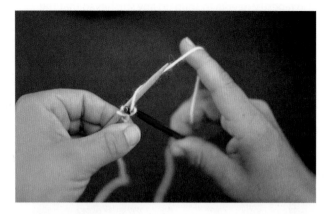

3. Bring yarn down between crochet hook and working needle.

Repeat steps 1–3 for desired number of stitches.

Three-Needle Bind-Off

Flip piece inside out. Hold needles so that LH and RH needles are parallel and are both held in LH. Insert DPN as if to knit into the first st on both needles simultaneously, and knit one stitch. Slip both sts off circular needle, one st is now on DPN. Repeat for second st, then pass first stitch on DPN over second stitch in normal BO procedure. Repeat process until all sts are bound off. Break yarn, weave through last st, and secure.

Wrap and Turn (W&T)

Wrap and turn for short-row shaping. *When next st is to be knit:* After working last st, with yarn in back sl next st purlwise onto RH needle. Move yarn to front then sl st back onto LH needle. Turn and work back as directed. *When next st is to be purled:* Follow directions above except begin with yarn in front and move it to back for wrap.

Zipper Installation

My preferred method of zipper installation is based on TECHKnitter's No-Sew Method.[1] This method, as indicated by its name, doesn't require a sewing machine or hand stitching and, instead, is based on making the zipper itself a knittable object. In order to use this method, you need a latch hook (also called a knit-picker), which is a tool that looks like a small crochet hook but opens and closes fully, making it perfect for bringing yarn from one side of a zipper to the other without it falling off the hook. You will also need some spare circular needles within a size or two of the needles used in your project. And, if you are working a project with bulky yarn (such as the Jake Jacket), you may want to seek a worsted weight yarn of similar shade (as I did) and use that for your installation instead of attempting to pull the bulky yarn through the zipper tape.

1. Measure your zipper and calculate the total number of stitches to pick up on it. Your zipper should match the length of the zipper band or be slightly shorter. Once you know the length of the zipper, plug this length into the Stitch Adjustment Worksheet and work calculations A to D to compute the total stitch count.

2. On the right side of the zipper, mark where each of your stitches will go. You can use a pencil for this or you can use a large (but sharp) needle. I prefer using a pencil because it usually takes me a couple of tries before I get the right number of stitches evenly spaced.

3. Insert the latch hook into the first hole *from right side to wrong side of the zipper. Place your yarn into the open latch hook, then close it, and pull the yarn through to the right side of the zipper, making a loop. Open the latch hook and release the yarn. Slide this stitch onto circular needle and pull the yarn snug on the needle. Insert the latch hook into the next hole and repeat from * until all of your stitches are on the needle.

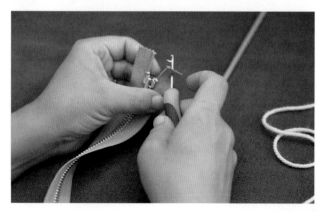

continued

1. "Zippers in knitwear, the no-sewing way." TECHknitting. October 22, 2012.
   http://techknitting.blogspot.com/2012/10/zipper-in-knitwear-no-sewing-way.html

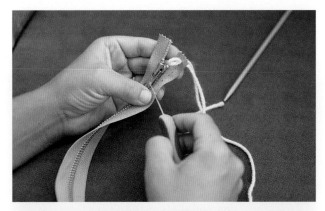

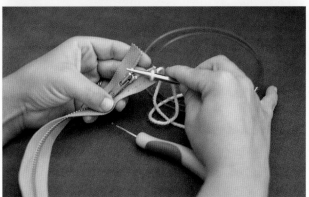

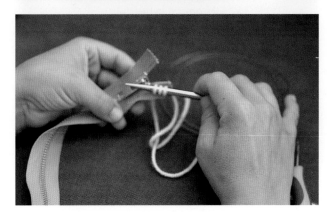

7. Repeat steps 5 and 6 to seam the other side of the zipper to your project.

This method of installation is definitely a bit more time-consuming than using a machine. But, considering the time you spent making your fabulous sweater, it is well worth the meticulous finishing effort. However, if you are more comfortable using your own installation method, go for it! If you've never installed a zipper before, this method is perfect for you and should make you feel comfortable and confident about working a project that calls for it.

4. Repeat steps 2 and 3 on the other side of the zipper. If you are working with a separating zipper, you may find it easier to separate the two pieces before picking up the second set of stitches.

5. Pick up and knit the same number of stitches along one side of the zipper band as you created on each side of the zipper.

6. Work a three-needle bind-off to seam the zipper to the zipper band.

Abbreviations

[ ]	rep instructions in brackets as many times as noted after
BO	bind off
CO	cast on
dec	decrease
DPN(s)	double-pointed needle(s)
EOR	every other round
est	established
inc	increase
k	knit
k2tog	knit 2 sts together
k3tog	knit 3 sts together
kf&b	knit into the front and back of the same stitch
LH	left hand
M1	make 1 st
M1L	make 1 left-leaning st
M1R	make 1 right-leaning st
p	purl
p2tog	purl 2 sts together
pat	pattern
pm	place marker
rep	repeat
rem	remaining
Rev St st	reverse stockinette stitch; purl all sts on the right side, knit all sts on the wrong side
RH	right hand

rnd	round
RS	right side
sl	slip
ssk	slip 1 st, slip 1 st, knit 2 sts together
sm	slip marker
st(s)	stitch(es)
St st	stockinette stitch; knit all sts on the right side, purl all sts on the wrong side
tbl	through the back loop
WS	wrong side
WYIF	With yarn in front
YFON	yarn forward over needle
yo	yarn over

Cable Stitches

X2	Crossover. Knit into second st on LH needle, do not slide off needle. Knit into first st on LH needle, slide both sts off needle.
C4B	Slip 2 sts to cable needle and hold to back, k2, k2 from cable needle.
C4F	Slip 2 sts to cable needle and hold to front, k2, k2 from cable needle.
T4B	Slip 2 sts to cable needle and hold to back, k2, p2 from cable needle.
T4F	Slip 2 sts to cable needle and hold to front, p2, k2 from cable needle.

Grow-with-Me Projects

ALL OF THE DESIGNS in this section incorporate at least one tip from the reference section for giving garments extra longevity. Most are also worked top-down which makes the length measurements versatile and adjustable either during your original knit or later on once the child starts to outgrow it. Check out how they work in practice by seeing some of the projects on different sized little men.

Charlie V

Think of this sweater as a template. It's a great first sweater with all the basic components. Add colorwork or stripes if you fancy or change the hem and cuffs. If you're feeling adventurous you can even change the neckline. Do whatever you want to make it his. Grow-with-Me Tip #3—the rolled hem—is featured here. It is one of my favorites and you'll see it a few other times as well. Because this sweater is worked top-down, the sleeves and body can be knit to the perfect length before binding off. Tucker is swinging in the size 6 and Charlie (three years younger) wore it on the cover.

Size

Standard Size: 4 (6, 8, 10, 12)
Finished Chest: 25 (27, 29, 31, 33)"/63.5 (68.5, 73.5, 79, 84) cm

Gauge

20 sts and 28 rows in St st = 4"/10 cm square

Yarn

560 (630, 750, 860, 970) yd./510 (575, 685, 785, 890) m worsted weight #4 yarn (shown in Lorna's Laces Shepherd Worsted; 100% merino; 225 yd./206 m per 4 oz./114 g skein; Pioneer)

Needles and Other Materials

- US 7 (4.5 mm) 24"/60 cm circular needle
- US 7 (4.5 mm) set of 5 double-pointed needles
- Stitch markers
- US G-6 (4 mm) crochet hook
- Yarn needle
- Scrap yarn and/or stitch holders

Pattern Notes

- Sweater is worked top-down with seamless raglan-style sleeves.

Body

With circular needles, crochet hook, and scrap yarn, provisionally CO 31 (35, 35, 39, 39) sts.
Row 1 (WS): P1 (2, 1, 2, 1), pm, p1, pm, p3, pm, p1, pm, p19 (21, 23, 25, 27), pm, p1, pm, p3, pm, p1, pm, p1 (2, 1, 2, 1).

INCREASES

Inc Row (RS): [K to marker, M1R, sm, k1, sm, M1L] 4 times, k to end of row—8 sts inc.

Purl 1 row.

Neckline Inc Row: K1, M1L, [K to marker, M1R, sm, k1, sm, M1L] 4 times, k to last st, M1R, k1—10 sts inc.

Purl 1 row.

Work last 4 rows a total of 8 (9, 10, 11, 12) times. Do not turn—175 (197, 215, 237, 255) sts: 51 (57, 63, 69, 75) back sts, 25 (29, 31, 35, 37) front sts, 35 (39, 43, 47, 51) sleeve sts, 4 raglan sts.

Place marker and join to work in the round, being careful not to twist sts. Knit 1 round.

Note: Inc Rnd is worked for the three smallest sizes only.

Inc Rnd: [K to marker, M1R, sm, k1, sm, M1L] 4 times, k to end of rnd—8 sts inc.

Work Inc Rnd every other rnd a total of 3 (1, 1, 0, 0) times—199 (205, 223, 237, 255) sts: 57 (59, 65, 69, 75) back sts, 56 (60, 64, 70, 74) front sts, 41 (41, 45, 47, 51) sleeve sts, 4 raglan sts.

Work even in St st until piece measures 5 (5.5, 6, 6.5, 7)"/13 (14, 15, 16, 17) cm from back neck CO edge.

SEPARATE SLEEVES FROM BODY

Next Rnd: [K to marker, remove marker, k1, remove marker, sl next 41 (41, 45, 47, 51) sleeve sts to holder, CO 4 (6, 6, 6, 6) sts, remove marker, k1, remove marker] twice, k to end of rnd—125 (135, 145, 155, 165) sts.

Work even in St st until piece measures 15.25 (16.5, 18.5, 20, 21)"/39 (42, 47, 51, 53) cm from back neck CO edge. BO all sts.

Sleeve (Make 2)

Note: Two additional sts are picked up than were CO at underarm to minimize holes. Make second sleeve same as first.

Place sts for sleeve on DPNs. With spare DPN and RS facing, starting at center underarm, pick up and knit 3 (4, 4, 4, 4) sts. Knit around 41 (41, 45, 47, 51) sleeve sts, pick up and knit 3 (4, 4, 4, 4) sts, place marker and join to work in the round—47 (49, 53, 55, 59) sts.

Knit in the round for 1"/2.5 cm.

Dec Rnd: K1, ssk, k to last 3 sts, k2tog, k1—2 sts dec.

Work Dec Rnd every 11 (11, 12, 13, 13) rnds a total of 7 (7, 7, 7, 8) times—33 (35, 39, 41, 43) sts.

Work even until sleeve measures 12.5 (13, 13.75, 15, 16.25)"/32 (33, 35, 38, 41) cm.

BO all sts.

Finishing

NECKLINE

Remove provisional CO and place sts on spare needle,
ready to work. Starting at center front, pick up and knit
27 (32, 36, 40, 44) sts on right front diagonal edge, knit
across 31 (35, 35, 39, 39) neckline sts, pick up and knit 27
(32, 36, 40, 44) sts on left front diagonal edge. Place
marker and join to work in the round—85 (99, 107, 119,
127) sts.

Dec Rib: P1, k2tog, *p1, k1; rep from * to last 3 sts, p1, ssk—
2 sts dec.

Work Dec Rib every rnd for a total of 4 rnds—77 (91, 99,
111, 119) sts.

BO all sts in rib with Jeny's Surprisingly Stretchy BO (see
page 28).

Weave in all loose ends. Block.

FINISHED MEASUREMENTS

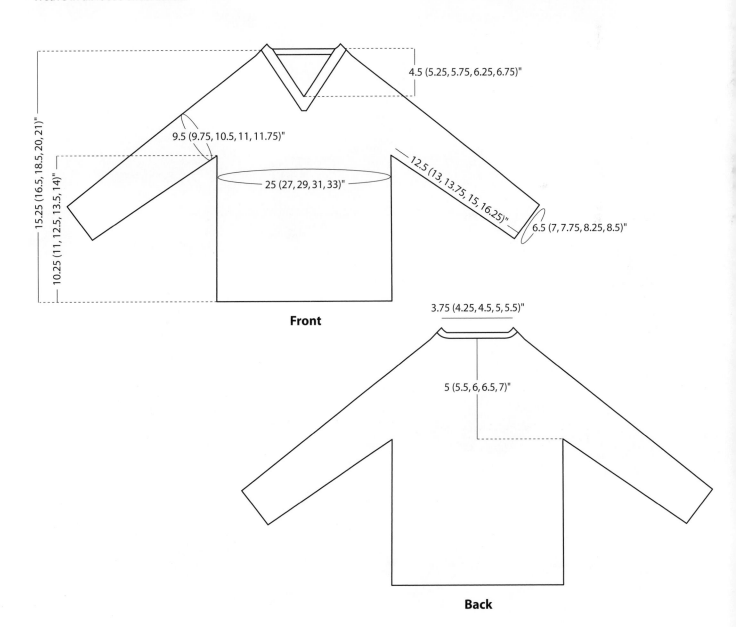

4.5 (5.25, 5.75, 6.25, 6.75)"

9.5 (9.75, 10.5, 11, 11.75)"

12.5 (13, 13.75, 15, 16.25)"

25 (27, 29, 31, 33)"

6.5 (7, 7.75, 8.25, 8.5)"

15.25 (16.5, 18.5, 20, 21)"

10.25 (11, 12.5, 13.5, 14)"

Front

3.75 (4.25, 4.5, 5, 5.5)"

5 (5.5, 6, 6.5, 7)"

Back

Striated Crew

This Grow-with-Me top features a colorblock inspired striping sequence and adjustable rolled hem and cuffs, just like in the Charlie V design. It is shown on two different models who are normally two sizes apart. Caden and Henry are wearing the size 8. It is shown in four colors; use as many or as few as you'd like.

Size

Standard Size: 4 (6, 8, 10, 12)
Finished Chest: 24.75 (27, 29.5, 31.25, 32.75)"/63 (68.5, 75, 79, 83) cm

Gauge

19 sts and 28 rows in St st = 4"/10 cm square

Yarn

Worsted weight #4 yarn [shown in Ewe Ewe Yarns Wooly Worsted; 100% merino; 95 yd./87 m per 1.8 oz./50 g skein; Sage (A), Wheat (B), Aqua (C), and Chocolate (D)]

- Color A: 350 (400, 450, 515, 585) yd./320 (370, 410, 470, 535) m
- Color B: 95 (110, 135, 150, 170) yd./90 (100, 125, 140, 155) m
- Color C: 65 (80, 100, 115, 130) yd./60 (75, 90, 105, 120) m
- Color D: 50 (60, 80, 95, 105) yd./45 (55, 75, 90, 100) m

Needles and Other Materials

- US 7 (4.5 mm) 24"/60 cm circular needle
- US 7 (4.5 mm) set of 5 double-pointed needles
- Stitch markers
- US G-6 (4 mm) crochet hook
- Yarn needle
- Scrap yarn and/or stitch holders

Pattern Notes

- Sweater is worked top-down with seamless raglan-style sleeves.

Stitch Guide

Striated Sequence
Note: Work first color changes as noted in pattern.
Work 12 rnds A.
Work 10 (12, 16, 18, 20) rnds D.
Work 14 (16, 20, 22, 24) rnds C.
Work 18 (20, 24, 26, 28) rnds B.
Work the rest in A.

Body

With circular needles, crochet hook, and scrap yarn, provisionally CO 35 (38, 40, 42, 42) sts. Switch to C.
Row 1 (WS): P1, pm, p1, pm, p4, pm, p1, pm, p21 (24, 26, 28, 28), pm, p1, pm, p4, pm, p1, pm, p1.

INCREASES

Inc Row: [K to marker, M1R, sm, k1, sm, M1L] 4 times, k to end of row—8 sts inc.
Purl 1 row.

Neckline Inc Row: K1, M1L, [K to marker, M1R, sm, k1, sm, M1L] 4 times, k to last st, M1R, k1—10 sts inc.

Purl 1 row.

Switch to B. Work last 4 rows once more—71 (74, 76, 78, 78) sts: 29 (32, 34, 36, 36) back sts, 7 front sts, 12 sleeve sts, 4 raglan sts.

Next Row: CO 15 (18, 20, 22, 22) sts, [k to marker, M1R, sm, k1, sm, M1L] twice, k to end of row, join to work in the round, being careful not to twist sts, [K to marker, M1R, sm, k1, sm, M1L] twice. Place marker for end of rnd—94 (100, 104, 108, 108) sts: 31 (34, 36, 38, 38) front/back sts, 14 sleeve sts, 4 raglan sts.

Knit 1 round.

Inc Rnd: [K to marker, M1R, sm, k1, sm, M1L] 4 times, k to end of rnd—8 sts inc.

Switch to A.

Work Inc Rnd every other rnd a total of 12 (13, 14, 15, 17) times and *at the same time* work Striated Sequence—190 (204, 216, 228, 244) sts: 55 (60, 64, 68, 72) front/back sts, 38 (40, 42, 44, 48) sleeve sts, 4 raglan sts.

Continue in Striated Sequence and *at the same time* separate body from sleeves when piece measures 5 (5.5, 6, 6.5, 7)"/13 (14, 15, 16.5, 18) cm from back neck CO edge.

SEPARATE BODY AND SLEEVES

Next Rnd: [K to marker, remove marker, k1, remove marker, sl next 40 (42, 44, 46, 50) sts to holder, CO 4 (4, 6, 6, 6) sts, remove marker, k1, remove marker] twice, k to end of rnd—118 (128, 140, 148, 156) sts.

Work even in Striated Sequence until piece measures 15.25 (16.5, 18.5, 20, 21)"/39 (42, 47, 51, 53) cm from back neck CO edge. BO all sts.

Sleeve (Make 2)

Note: Match striping sequence to body. The total number of sts picked up for the underarm are 2 more than were cast on for the body to minimize holes. Make second sleeve same as first.

Place sts for sleeve on DPNs. With spare DPN and RS facing, starting at center underarm, pick up and knit 3 (3, 4, 4, 4) sts, knit around 40 (42, 44, 46, 50) sleeve sts, pick up and knit 3 (3, 4, 4, 4) sts, place marker and join to work in the round—46 (48, 52, 54, 58) sts.

Knit in the round for 1"/2.5 cm.

Dec Rnd: K1, ssk, k to last 3 sts, k2tog, k1—2 sts dec.

Work Dec Rnd every 10 rnds a total of 6 (6, 7, 7, 8) times—34 (36, 38, 40, 42) sts.

Work even until sleeve measures 11.75 (12, 12.75, 14, 15.5)"/30 (30.5, 32, 35.5, 39) cm.

BO all sts.

Finishing

NECKLINE

Remove provisional CO and place sts on needles, ready to
work RS. With A, knit across 35 (38, 40, 42, 42) neckline sts,
pick up and knit 7 sts along left front edge, 15 (18, 20, 22,
22) sts along center front CO edge, 7 sts along right front
edge, pm for end of rnd—64 (70, 74, 78, 78) sts.
Rib: *K1, p1; rep from * around.
Work in rib for 5 rounds.
BO all sts.
Weave in all loose ends. Block.

FINISHED MEASUREMENTS

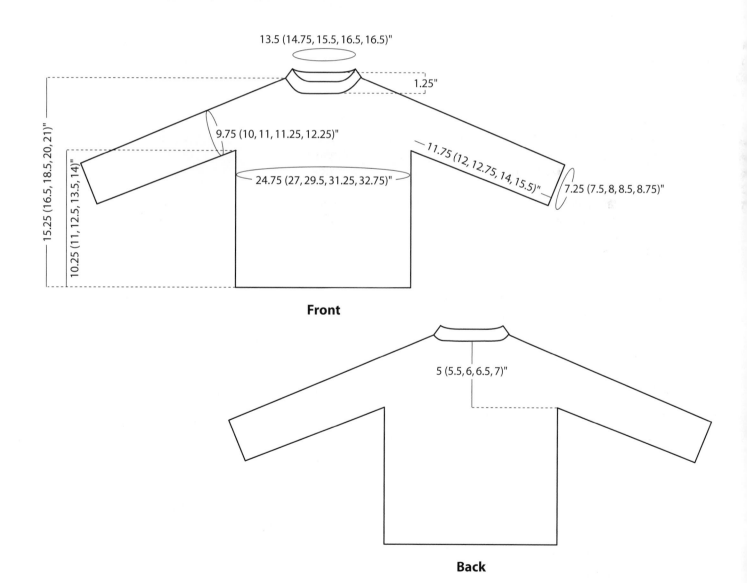

13.5 (14.75, 15.5, 16.5, 16.5)"

1.25"

9.75 (10, 11, 11.25, 12.25)"

11.75 (12, 12.75, 14, 15.5)"

15.25 (16.5, 18.5, 20, 21)"

10.25 (11, 12.5, 13.5, 14)"

24.75 (27, 29.5, 31.25, 32.75)"

7.25 (7.5, 8, 8.5, 8.75)"

Front

5 (5.5, 6, 6.5, 7)"

Back

Boy Tee

This easy V-neck tee is lightweight, breezy, and easily adjustable. Worked in fingering weight yarn, it's perfect for mild weather and transitioning seasons. Short sleeves and an extra-long body will make this sweater last. Jake is splashing around in the size 4.

Size

Standard Size: 4 (6, 8, 10, 12)
Finished Chest: 26 (28, 29.25, 31.25, 33.25)"/66 (71, 74, 79, 84.5) cm

Gauge

24 sts and 36 rows in St st = 4"/10 cm square

Yarn

Fingering weight #1 yarn [shown in Spud and Chloë Fine; 80% superwash wool, 20% silk; 248 yd./227 m per 2.3 oz./65 g skein; Shitake (A) and Calypso (B)]
- Color A: 525 (600, 715, 820, 910) yd./480 (550, 650, 750, 830) m
- Color B: 85 (90, 95, 100, 105) yd./77 (82, 86, 91, 96) m

Needles and Other Materials:

- US 3 (3.25 mm) 24"/60 cm circular needle
- US 3 (3.25 mm) set of 5 double-pointed needles
- Stitch markers
- US D-3 (3.25 mm) crochet hook
- Yarn needle
- Scrap yarn and/or stitch holders

Pattern Notes

- Sweater is worked top-down with seamless raglan-style sleeves.
- The pocket is knit separately and stitched onto the garment.

Body

With circular needles, scrap yarn, and crochet hook, provisionally CO 48 (50, 50, 54, 56) sts. Switch to A.
Set-up Row (WS): P2, pm, p1, pm, p6 (6, 6, 7, 7), pm, p1, pm, p28 (30, 30, 32, 34), pm, p1, pm, p6 (6, 6, 7, 7), pm, p1, pm, p2.

INCREASES

Inc Row: K1, M1L, [k to marker, M1R, sm, k1, sm, M1L] 4 times, k to last st, M1R, k1—10 sts inc.
Purl 1 row.
Work Inc Row every RS row a total of 12 (13, 13, 14, 15) times and *do not turn*—168 (180, 180, 194, 206) sts: 52

(56, 56, 60, 64) back sts, 30 (32, 32, 35, 37) sleeve sts, 26 (28, 28, 30, 32) front sts, 4 raglan sts.
Place marker, and join to work in the round. Marker is at center front of V-neck. Knit 1 round.
Inc Rnd: [K to marker, M1R, sm, k1, sm, M1L] 4 times, k to end of rnd—8 sts inc.
Work Inc Rnd every other rnd a total of 9 (10, 12, 12, 13) times—240 (260, 276, 290, 310) sts: 70 (76, 80, 84, 90) back/front sts, 48 (52, 56, 59, 63) sleeve sts, 4 raglan sts.
Work even until sweater measures 5 (5.5, 6, 6.5, 7)"/13 (14, 15, 16.5, 18) cm from back neck CO edge.

SEPARATE BODY AND SLEEVES

Remove markers during the next round, except for end of round marker.

Next Rnd: [K to marker, k1, slip next 48 (52, 56, 59, 63) sleeve sts to scrap yarn and place on hold, cable CO 6 (6, 6, 8, 8) sts, k1] twice, k to end of rnd—156 (168, 176, 188, 200) sts.

Knit in the round until sweater measures 14.75 (16, 18, 19.5, 20.5)"/37.5 (41, 46, 49.5, 52) cm from back neck CO edge. Break yarn. Switch to B.

Knit in the round for 1"/2.5 cm. BO all sts.

Sleeve (Make 2)

Note: Two additional sts are picked up than were CO at under-arm to minimize holes. Make second sleeve same as first.

Place 48 (52, 56, 59, 63) sleeve sts on DPNs, ready to work RS. Starting at center underarm, with spare DPN and A, pick up and knit 4 (4, 4, 5, 5) sts, knit across sleeve sts, pick up and knit 4 (4, 4, 5, 5) sts, pm, and join to work in the round—56 (60, 64, 69, 73) sts.

Knit in the round for 2.5 (2.5, 3, 3, 3)"/6 (6, 7.5, 7.5, 7.5) cm. Break yarn. Switch to B. Knit in the round for 1"/2.5 cm. BO all sts.

Finishing

POCKET

With B and spare DPN, CO 15 (15, 17, 19, 21) sts, leaving a long tail for sewing.

Work in St st for 2"/5 cm, ending after a WS row.

Dec Row (RS): K1, ssk, k to last 3 sts, k2tog, k1—2 sts dec.

Work Dec Row every RS row a total of 5 (5, 6, 7, 8) times—5 sts.

Next Row (WS): P1, p3tog, p1.

Next Row: K3tog.

Break yarn, weave through rem st and secure. Allow CO edge to roll slightly, matching cuffs and hem, then use CO tail to stitch patch pocket onto left front of sweater as shown.

NECKLINE

Remove provisional CO and place sts on spare needle, ready to work. Starting at center front, pick up and knit 24 (26, 26, 28, 30) sts on right front diagonal edge, knit across 48 (50, 50, 54, 56) neckline sts, pick up and knit 24 (26, 26, 28, 30) sts on left front diagonal edge. Place marker and join to work in the round—96 (102, 102, 110, 116) sts.

Dec Rib: P1, k2tog, *p1, k1; rep from * to last 3 sts, p1, ssk— 2 sts dec.

Work Dec Rib every rnd for a total of 4 rnds—88 (94, 94, 102, 108) sts.

BO all sts in rib with Jeny's Surprisingly Stretchy BO (see page 28).

Weave in all loose ends. Block.

FINISHED MEASUREMENTS

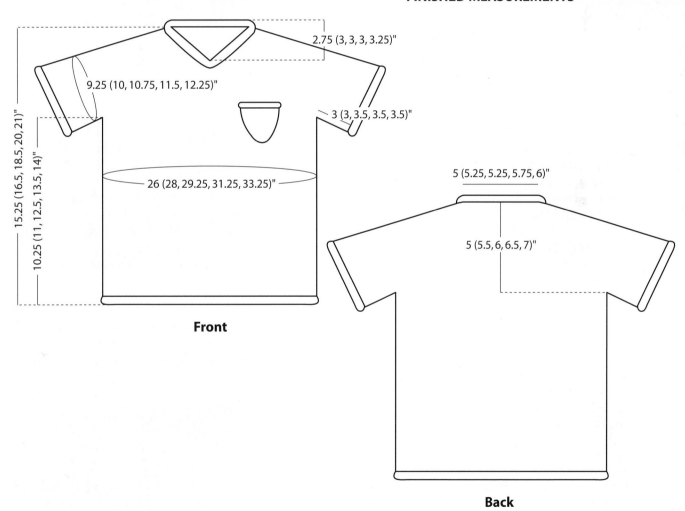

2.75 (3, 3, 3, 3.25)"

9.25 (10, 10.75, 11.5, 12.25)"

3 (3, 3.5, 3.5, 3.5)"

15.25 (16.5, 18.5, 20, 21)"

10.25 (11, 12.5, 13.5, 14)"

26 (28, 29.25, 31.25, 33.25)"

Front

5 (5.25, 5.25, 5.75, 6)"

5 (5.5, 6, 6.5, 7)"

Back

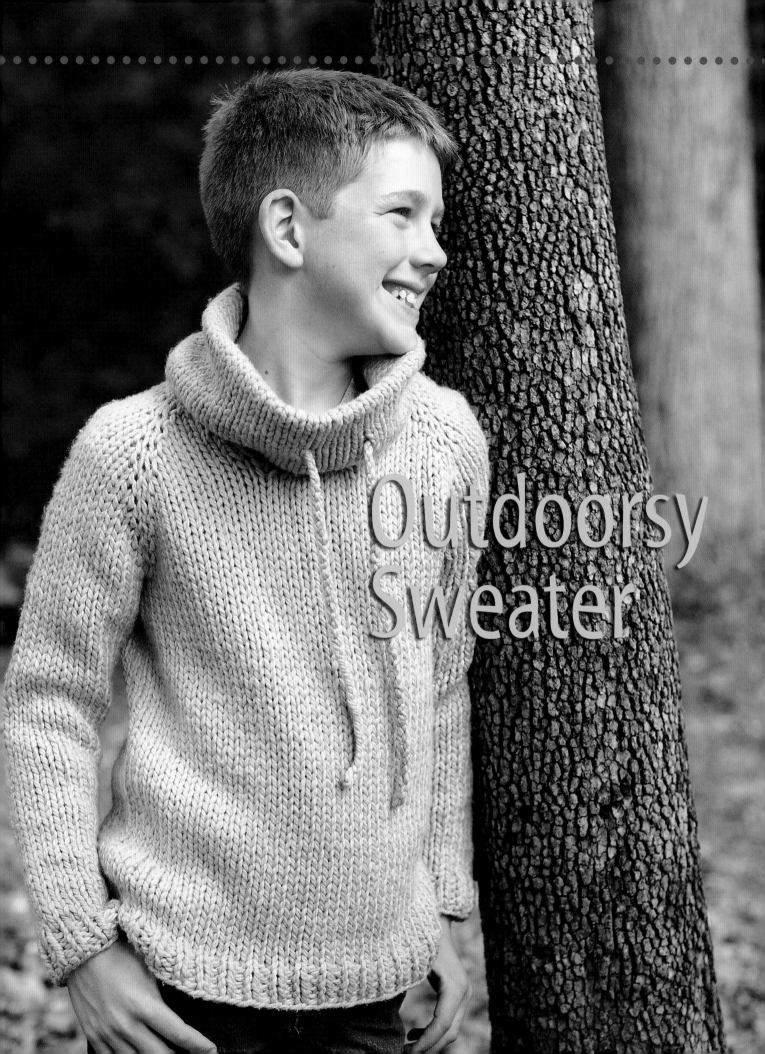

Outdoorsy Sweater

A rough and tumble boy may not appreciate intricate colorwork or cables, but he definitely wants something to keep him warm. This project does just that—it's a basic sweater with a modern neckline to set it apart. It is created with extra ease to allow him the greatest freedom of motion for his outdoor adventures and to help it last a little longer. Because it is worked top-down, you can easily remove the original hem and cuffs to take advantage of Grow-with-Me Tip #2. Charlie was nice and cozy in the size 10.

Size
Standard Size: 4 (6, 8, 10, 12)
Finished Chest: 25.5 (28, 29.5, 32, 33.5)"/65 (71, 75, 81, 85) cm

Gauge
10 sts and 14 rows in St st = 4"/10 cm square

Yarn
375 (425, 475, 550, 600) yd./340 (390, 435, 500, 550) m bulky weight #6 yarn (shown in Spud and Chloë Outer; 65% wool, 35% organic cotton; 60 yd./55 m per 3.5 oz./100 g skein; Sandbox)

Needles and Other Materials
- US 11 (8 mm) 24"/60 cm circular needle
- US 11 (8 mm) set of 5 double-pointed needles
- Stitch markers
- US L-11 (8 mm) crochet hook
- Large safety pin
- Scrap yarn and/or stitch holders
- Yarn needle

Pattern Notes
- Sweater is worked top-down with seamless raglan-style sleeves.
- Collar is knit separately and then seamlessly attached.

Body

With circular needles, crochet hook, and scrap yarn, provisionally CO 19 (20, 23, 24, 24) sts.
Row 1 (WS): P1, pm, p1, pm, p1 (1, 2, 2, 2), pm, p1, pm, p11 (12, 13, 14, 14), pm, p1, pm, p1 (1, 2, 2, 2), pm, p1, pm, p1.

INCREASES
Inc Row: [K to marker, M1R, sm, k1, sm, M1L] 4 times, k to end of row—8 sts inc.
Purl 1 row.
Neckline Inc Row: K1, M1L, [K to marker, M1R, sm, k1, sm, M1L] 4 times, k to last st, M1R, k1—10 sts inc.
Purl 1 row.

Work last 4 rows a total of 3 times and *do not turn*—73 (74, 77, 78, 78) sts: 23 (24, 25, 26, 26) back sts, 10 front sts, 13 (13, 14, 14, 14) sleeve sts, 4 raglan sts.
CO 3 (4, 5, 6, 6) sts, join to work in the round, knit to fourth marker, pm for end of rnd—76 (78, 82, 84, 84) sts: 23 (24, 25, 26, 26) back/front sts, 13 (13, 14, 14, 14) sleeve sts, 4 raglan sts.
Knit 1 round.

Inc Rnd: [M1L, k to marker, M1R, sm, k1, sm] 4 times, k to end of rnd—8 sts inc.

Work Inc Rnd every other rnd a total of 3 (4, 4, 5, 6) times—100 (110, 114, 124, 132) sts: 29 (32, 33, 36, 38) front/back sts, 19 (21, 22, 24, 26) sleeve sts, 4 raglan sts.

Work even in St st until sweater measures 5 (5.5, 6, 6.5, 7)"/13 (14, 15, 16.5, 18) cm from back neck CO edge.

SEPARATE BODY AND SLEEVES

Note: Remove raglan markers during the next round. Raglan sts will be slipped to holder for sleeves.

Next Rnd: [K to marker, sl next 21 (23, 24, 26, 28) sts to holder, CO 3 (3, 4, 4, 4) sts] twice, k to end of rnd—64 (70, 74, 80, 84) sts.

Work even in St st until piece measures 13.25 (14.5, 16.5, 18, 19)"/33.5 (37, 42, 46, 48) cm from back neck CO edge.

Rib: *K1, p1; rep from * around.

Work in Rib for 1"/2.5 cm. BO all sts.

Sleeve (Make 2)

Note: Two additional sts are picked up than were CO at under-arm to minimize holes. Make second sleeve same as first.

Place sts for sleeve on DPNs. With spare DPN and RS facing, starting at center underarm, pick up and knit 2 (2, 3, 3, 3) sts, knit around 21 (23, 24, 26, 28) sleeve sts, pick up and knit 3 sts, place marker and join to work in the round—26 (28, 30, 32, 34) sts.

Knit in the round for 1"/2.5 cm.

Dec Rnd: K1, ssk, k to last 3 sts, k2tog, k1—2 sts dec.

Work Dec Rnd every 7 rnds a total of 5 (5, 6, 6, 6) times—16 (18, 18, 20, 22) sts.

Work even until sleeve measures 11.25 (11.5, 12.5, 13.75, 15.25)"/28.5 (29, 32, 35, 39) cm.

Rib: *K1, p1; rep from * around.

Work in Rib for 1"/2.5 cm. BO all sts.

Finishing

COLLAR

With circular needle, CO 46 (48, 52, 54, 54) sts. Place marker and join to work in the round, being careful not to twist sts. Knit in the round until piece measures 7.5"/19 cm from CO edge.

Joining Rnd: Fold the knit section in half. Join working sts to CO edge as follows: * with left needle, pick up the first st from the CO edge and knit tog with next working st; rep from * to end of rnd.

Slip to spare circular needle and set aside.

NECKLINE

Remove provisional CO and place sts on circular needle. At the end of the row and with RS facing, pick up and knit 12 sts along left front diagonal edge, 3 (4, 5, 6, 6) sts along center front CO edge, and 12 sts along right front diagonal edge—46 (48, 52, 54, 54) sts.

Use three-needle bind-off (see page 30) to join Neckline and Collar sts.

With crochet hook, chain for 44"/112 cm and fasten off. Attach safety pin to one end of chain. Weave end of chain into front collar, .5" to the left of center. Use safety pin to string it around back of collar and again through the front of collar .5" to the right of center. Remove pin.

Weave in all loose ends. Block.

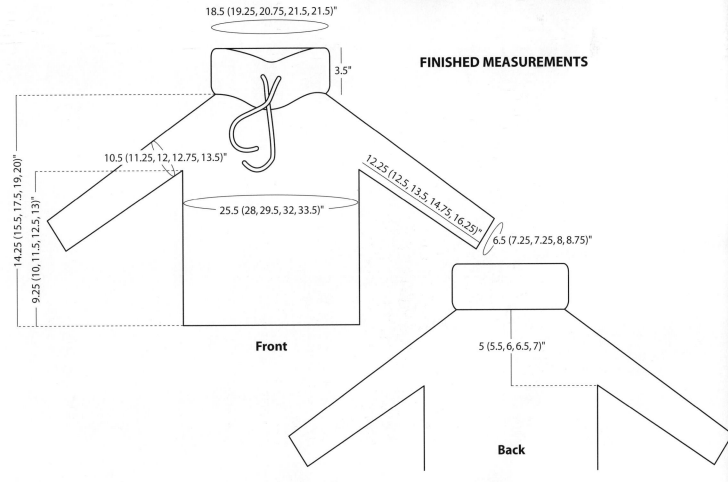

FINISHED MEASUREMENTS

18.5 (19.25, 20.75, 21.5, 21.5)"

3.5"

14.25 (15.5, 17.5, 19, 20)"

9.25 (10, 11.5, 12.5, 13)"

10.5 (11.25, 12, 12.75, 13.5)"

25.5 (28, 29.5, 32, 33.5)"

12.25 (12.5, 13.5, 14.75, 16.25)"

6.5 (7.25, 7.25, 8, 8.75)"

Front

5 (5.5, 6, 6.5, 7)"

Back

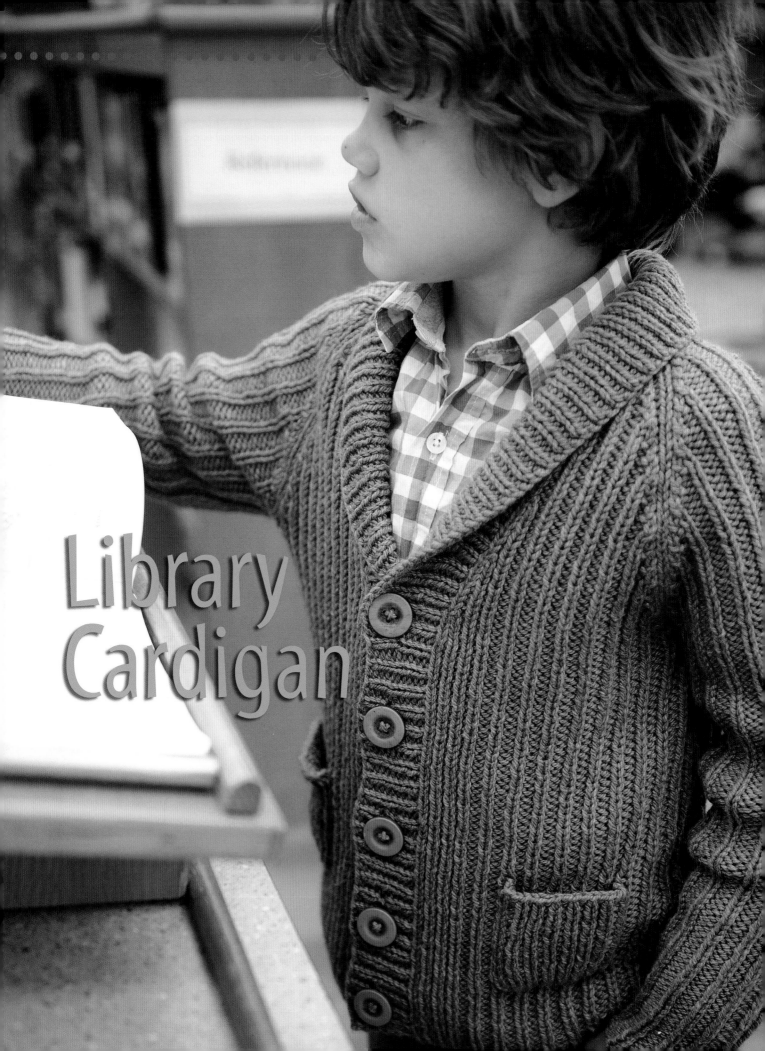

Library
Cardigan

*D*on't these boys look so handsome in this studious sweater? Benson, Charlie, and Jesse are all wearing a size 8. Charlie is five years old and Jesse and Benson are seven. The stretchy rib on this design makes it particularly grow-able and the cuffs can be folded up to fit shorter arms. It is just as charming worn oversized as it is fitted. This sweater features Grow-with-Me Tips #5 and #8.

Size

Standard Size: 4 (6, 8, 10, 12)
Finished Chest (buttoned): 25 (27.25, 29.25, 31.5, 33.75)"/63.5 (69, 74, 80, 86) cm

Gauge

22 sts and 25 rows in Rib on larger needles = 4"/10 cm square

Yarn

550 (625, 750, 875, 1000) yd./500 (570, 685, 800, 914) m light worsted weight #3 yarn (shown in Spud and Chloë Sweater; 55% wool, 45% organic cotton; 160 yd./146 m per 3.5 oz./100 g skein; Chocolate Milk)

Needles and Other Materials

- US 6 (4 mm) 24"/60 cm circular needle
- US 7 (4.5 mm) 24"/60 cm circular needle
- US 6 (4 mm) set of 5 double-pointed needles
- US 7 (4.5 mm) set of 5 double-pointed needles
- Awl or leather hole punch
- 4 (5, 5, 6, 6) 1"/2.5 cm buttons (shown with Renaissance)
- Scraps of leather for patches
- 90"/230 cm of leather thread for sewing

Pattern Notes

- Sweater is worked top-down with raglan-style seamless sleeves.
- Collar is picked up and knit and then shaped with short rows.
- Pockets are knit separately and stitched on.

Sleeve (Make 2)

With smaller DPNs, CO 24 (26, 30, 30, 32) sts. Place marker and join to work in the round, being careful not to twist sts.

Rib: K2, *p2, k1, rep from * to last 4 (3, 4, 4, 3) sts, p2, k to end of rnd.

Work in Rib until piece measures 1.5 (1.5, 1.5, 2, 2)"/4 (4, 4, 5, 5) cm from CO edge.

Inc Rnd: K1, M1L, work sts as they appear to last st, M1R, k1—2 sts inc.

Work Inc Rnd every 3 rnds a total of 12 (12, 12, 14, 14) times, keeping first 2 and last 2 sts in St st, and working all middle sts into p2, k1 rib pattern as they are added—48 (50, 54, 58, 60) sts.

Work in pat until sleeve measures 11.75 (12, 12.75, 14.5, 15.5)"/30 (30.5, 32, 37, 39) cm from CO edge.

Next row: Work in pat to last 4 (4, 4, 5, 5) sts. Sl next 8 (8, 8, 10, 10) sts (removing marker) to scrap yarn. Place rem 40 (42, 46, 48, 50) sts on hold and set aside.

Dec Row (RS): K1, ssk, [work in pat to 2 sts before marker, ssk, sm, k1, sm, k2tog] 4 times, work in pat to last 3 sts, k2tog, k1—10 sts dec.

Purl 1 row.

Raglan Dec Row (RS): [Work in pat to 2 sts before marker, ssk, sm, k1, sm, k2tog] 4 times, work in pat to end of row—8 sts dec.

Purl 1 row.

Work last 4 rows a total of 8 (9, 10, 11, 11) times—49 (47, 49, 43, 59) sts: 27 (29, 31, 31, 37) back sts, 6 (4, 4, 2, 4) sleeve sts, 3 (3, 3, 2, 5) front sts, 4 raglan sts.

Sizes 4, 6, 8, 12 only: Work Raglan Dec Row once more—41 (39, 41, 43, 51) sts: 25 (27, 29, 31, 35) back sts, 4 (2, 2, 2, 2) sleeve sts, 2 (2, 2, 2, 4) front sts, 4 raglan sts.

Place sts on hold for collar.

Collar

With RS facing and smaller needles, starting at bottom right front, pick up 3 sts for every 4 rows on vertical section before decreases begin, pick up 1 st for every row along diagonal neckline, pm, knit across sts on hold for collar, pm, pick up sts for left front as for right, ending with an odd-numbered total st count.

Row 1 (WS): P1, *k1, p1; repeat from * to end, slipping markers.

Body

With circular needle, CO 129 (141, 153, 165, 177) sts.

Next Row (WS): P2, [k1, p1] 3 times, *k2, p1; rep from * to last 10 sts, k2, [p1, k1] 3 times, p2.

Next Row (RS): K2, [p1, k1] 3 times, *p2, k1; rep from * to last 10 sts, p2, [k1, p1] 3 times, k2.

Work as est until sweater measures 9 (9.5, 10.75, 12, 12.75)"/23 (24, 27, 30.5, 32) cm from CO edge, ending after a WS row.

JOIN BODY AND SLEEVES

Work 27 (30, 33, 35, 38) sts in pat, *sl next 8 (8, 8, 10, 10) sts to scrap yarn and place on hold, pm, work sleeve sts in pat, pm,** work 59 (65, 71, 75, 81) back sts in pat, work from * to ** once more, work in pat to end of row—193 (209, 229, 241, 257) sts: 27 (30, 33, 35, 38) front sts, 40 (42, 46, 48, 50) sleeve sts, 59 (65, 71, 75, 81) back sts.

Next row (WS): *Work in pat to marker, sm, p1, pm, work in pat to one st before marker, pm, p1, sm; rep from * once more, work in pat to end of row.

Short-Row Collar Shaping

Note: Work in rib as set, picking up wraps on return rows.

Short Rows 1–2: Work to 2nd marker, W&T, work to marker, W&T.

Short Rows 3–4: Work to marker, sm, work 6 more sts, W&T, work to second marker, sm, work 6 more sts, W&T.

Short Rows 5–6: Work to second marker, sm, work 12 more sts, W&T, work to second marker, sm, work 12 more sts, W&T.

Short Rows 7–8: Work to second marker, sm, work 18 more sts, W&T, work to second marker, sm, work 18 more sts, W&T.

Short Rows 9–11: Work to second marker, sm, work 24 more sts, W&T, work to second marker, sm, work 24 more sts, W&T, continue in pat to end of row.

Short Rows 12–14: Work to second marker, sm, work 30 more sts, W&T, work to second marker, sm, work 30 more sts, W&T, continue in pat to end of row.

Short Rows 15–17: Work to second marker, sm, work 36 more sts, W&T, work to second marker, sm, work 36 more sts, W&T, continue in pat to end of row.

Next row (WS): Work in pat, picking up remaining wraps and removing markers.

Buttonhole row: Place markers for buttonholes 1"/2.5 cm from the CO edge at left front and 10"/ 25 cm from CO edge, with 2 (3, 3, 4, 4) markers spaced evenly in between.

Work in pattern, working a one-row three-stitch buttonhole (see page 29) at each marker.

Work 3 more rows in rib. BO loosely in rib.

Finishing

POCKET (Make 2)

Using 2 DPNs as straight needles, CO 17 sts, leaving a long tail for sewing.

Row 1 (WS): P1, *k1, p1; repeat from * to end of row.

Work in rib as est until pocket measures 3 (3, 3, 4, 4)"/7.5 (7.5, 7.5, 10, 10) cm.

BO all sts.

Using CO tail, sew patch pocket on each front. Graft underarms with Kitchener stitch (see page 28). Attach buttons to right front, corresponding with buttonholes on left front. Weave in all loose ends. Block. Follow instructions for elbow patches and attach after blocking.

ELBOW PATCHES

Trace template onto a separate piece of paper and cut out oval. Use it to cut out two leather patches. Do not cut out the circles inside the oval. Holding oval in line on top of cut out leather patch, use leather tool (either awl or punch) to create holes around perimeter of patch. You can punch through the paper and the leather simultaneously. Determine placement of patches on sweater, preferably by trying garment on recipient. Use 45"/114 cm length of leather cord to sew each patch onto a sweater sleeve.

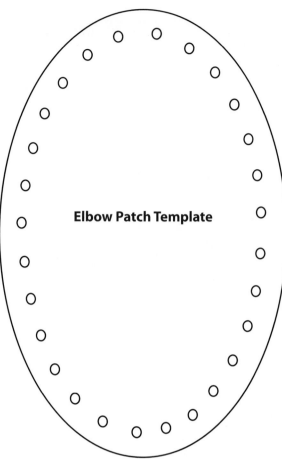

Elbow Patch Template

FINISHED MEASUREMENTS

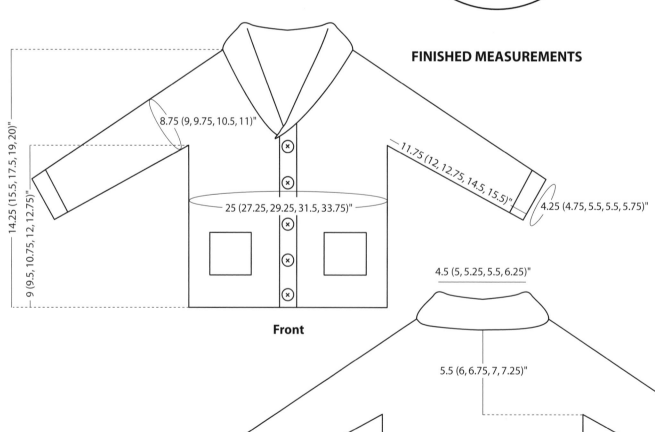

8.75 (9, 9.75, 10.5, 11)"

11.75 (12, 12.75, 14.5, 15.5)"

4.25 (4.75, 5.5, 5.5, 5.75)"

14.25 (15.5, 17.5, 19, 20)"

9 (9.5, 10.75, 12, 12.75)"

25 (27.25, 29.25, 31.5, 33.75)"

Front

4.5 (5, 5.25, 5.5, 6.25)"

5.5 (6, 6.75, 7, 7.25)"

Back

Long
John
PJs

nlike other designs in this book, there is no ease in this design because it is intended to be worn either for layering or as pajamas. However, it features a stretchy waffle knit pattern (Grow-with-Me Tip #8) so you don't have to worry about it being outgrown overly quickly. Still, size up if you'd rather it be worn as an outer layer or just don't want as snug of a fit. Charlie is reading to his baby brothers in the size 6.

TOP

Size

Standard Size: 4 (6, 8, 10, 12)
Finished Chest: 23 (25, 27.25, 29.25, 31.25)"/58.5 (63.5, 69, 74, 79) cm

Gauge

23 sts and 32 rows in St st = 4"/10 cm square

Yarn

460 (540, 640, 740, 840) yd./420 (500, 585, 680, 770) m sport weight #2 yarn (shown in Lorna's Laces Sportmate; 70% merino, 30% viscose; 270 yd./247 m per 3.5 oz./100 g skein; Cedar)

Needles and Other Materials

- US 5 (3.75 mm) 24"/60 cm circular needle
- US 5 (3.75 mm) set of 5 double-pointed needles
- Stitch markers
- Yarn needle
- Scrap yarn and/or stitch holders

BOTTOMS

Size

Standard Size: 4 (6, 8, 10, 12)
Finished Waist: 19.5 (20.25, 20.75, 22, 23)"/49.5 (51.5, 53, 56, 58.5) cm

Gauge

23 sts and 32 rows in St st on larger needles = 4"/10 cm square

Yarn

500 (575, 660, 750, 860) yd./460 (525, 600, 685, 785) m sport weight #2 yarn (shown in Lorna's Laces Sportmate; 70% merino, 30% viscose; 270 yd./247 m per 3.5 oz./100 g skein; Cedar)

Needles and Other Materials

- US 4 (3.5 mm) 16"/40 cm circular needle
- US 5 (3.75 mm) 16"/40 cm circular needle
- US 5 (3.75 mm) set of 5 double-pointed needles
- Stitch markers
- Yarn needle
- Scrap yarn and/or stitch holders
- 1"/2.5 cm elastic measuring for finished waist
- Sewing needle and thread to secure elastic

Pattern Notes:

- Top is worked bottom-up with raglan-style seamless sleeves.
- Pants are knit in the round from the waist down with short-row shaping at the rear and side shaping for the hips. Each leg is worked separately in the round.
- Choose the size that is equal to or smaller than your child's measurements.

Stitch Guide

Waffle Pattern (worked in the round over a multiple of 3 sts)

Rnds 1–3: *K2, p1; rep from * around.
Rnd 4: Purl.
Rep 4 rnds for pattern.

Top

SLEEVE (Make 2)

With DPNs, CO 28 (28, 31, 31, 34) sts. Place marker and join to work in the round, being careful not to twist sts.

Rnds 1–3: K1, *k1, p1, k1; rep from * to end of rnd.

Rnd 4: K1, purl to last st, k1.

Repeat Rnds 1–4 once more.

Inc Rnd: K1, M1L, work in pat to last st, M1R, k1—2 sts inc.

Next Rnd: K1, work in Waffle Pattern to last 2 sts, k2.

Work in Waffle Pattern as est and *at the same time* work Inc Rnd every 8 rnds a total of 7 (9, 9, 10, 10) times, adjusting increased st to pattern on the following rnd—42 (46, 49, 51, 54) sts.

Work even until sleeve measures 12.75 (13.25, 14, 15, 16.25)"/32 (33.5, 35.5, 38, 41) cm from CO edge.

Next Rnd: Work to last 4 sts, sl next 4 (6, 6, 8, 8) sts (removing marker) to scrap yarn for underarm, noting which rnd of Waffle Pattern was completed last—38 (40, 43, 43, 46) sts.

Place sleeve sts on hold. Repeat for second sleeve.

BODY

With larger circular needles, CO 132 (144, 156, 168, 180) sts. Place marker and join to work in the round, being careful not to twist sts.

Work in Waffle Pattern until sweater measures 9.5 (10.5, 12, 13, 13.5)"/24 (27, 30.5, 33, 34) cm, ending after working same rnd in pattern as for sleeves.

Joining Body and Sleeves

Next Rnd: Work in pat for 30 (32, 35, 37, 40) sts, *pm, k1, sl next 4 (6, 6, 8, 8) sts to holder for underarm, pm, knit 38 (40, 43, 43, 46) sleeve sts, pm, k1 from body, pm**, k60 (64, 70, 74, 80), rep from * to **, work in pat to end of rnd—200 (212, 230, 238, 256) sts: 60 (64, 70, 74, 80) front/back sts, 38 (40, 43, 43, 46) sleeve sts, 4 raglan sts.

Work 2 (2, 4, 8, 8) rnds in pattern.

Dec Rnd: [Work in pat to 2 sts before marker, ssk, sm, k1, sm, k2tog] 4 times, work to end of rnd—8 sts dec.

Work Dec Rnd every other rnd a total of 7 (8, 9, 9, 11) times—144 (148, 158, 166, 168) sts: 46 (48, 52, 56, 58) front/back sts, 24 (24, 25, 25, 24) sleeve sts, 4 raglan sts.

Discontinue Waffle Pattern and complete sweater in St st.

Work Dec Rnd every other rnd a total of 3 more times—120 (124, 134, 142, 144) sts: 40 (42, 46, 50, 52) front/back sts, 18 (18, 19, 19, 18) sleeve sts, 4 raglan sts.

Next Rnd: K to fourth marker, k14, sl next 12 (14, 18, 22, 24) sts to holder for front collar—108 (110, 116, 120, 120) sts: 40 (42, 46, 50, 52) back sts, 14 front sts, 18 (18, 19, 19, 18) sleeve sts, 4 raglan sts.

Remainder of sweater will be worked back and forth.

Turn, purl 1 row, removing end of rnd marker at center back (fifth marker) but leaving raglan markers in place.

Neckline Dec Row: K1, ssk, [k to 2 sts before marker, ssk, sm, k1, sm, k2tog] 4 times, k to last 3 sts, k2tog, k1—10 sts dec.
Next Row: Purl.
Raglan Dec Row: [K to 2 sts before marker, ssk, sm, k1, sm, k2tog] 4 times, k to end of row—8 sts dec.
Next Row: Purl.
Work last 4 rows 4 times—36 (38, 44, 48, 48) sts: 24 (26, 30, 34, 36) back sts, 2 front sts, 2 (2, 3, 3, 2) sleeve sts, 4 raglan sts.

Finishing

Neckline

Knit across 36 (38, 44, 48, 48) back neck sts, pick up and knit 14 sts along diagonal left front edge, knit across 12 (14, 18, 22, 24) sts at center front, pick up and knit 14 sts along diagonal right front edge, place marker and join to work in the round—76 (80, 90, 98, 100) sts.
Rib: *K1, p1; rep from * around.
Work in Rib for 5 rounds. BO all sts with Jeny's Surprisingly Stretchy BO (see page 28).
Graft underarm sts with Kitchener Stitch (see page 28). Weave in all loose ends. Block.

FINISHED MEASUREMENTS

13.25 (14, 15.75, 17, 17.5)"

7.25 (8, 8.5, 8.75, 9.5)"

14.25 (15.5, 17.5, 19, 20)"

9.5 (10.5, 12, 13, 13.5)"

23 (25, 27.25, 29.25, 31.25)"

12.75, 13.25, 14, 15, 16.25)"

4.75 (4.75, 5.5, 5.5, 6)"

Front

4.75 (5, 5.5, 6, 6.5)"

Back

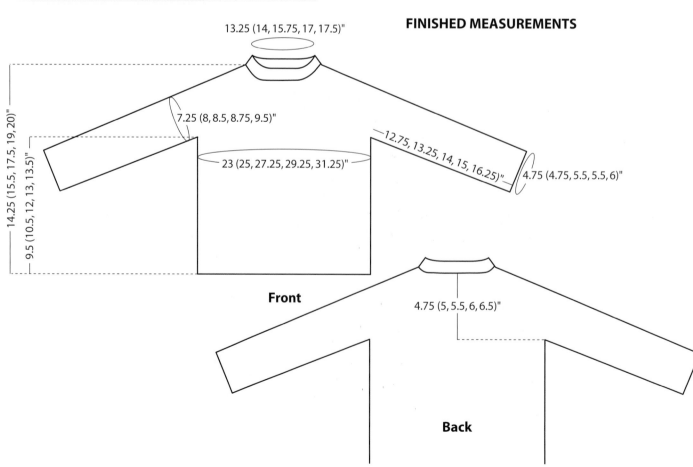

Bottoms

WAIST AND HIP SHAPING

With smaller circular needle, CO 112 (116, 120, 124, 132) sts.
Place marker and join to work in the round, being careful
not to twist sts. .

Rib: *K1, p1; rep from * around.

Work in Rib for 1"/2.5 cm. Purl one row (turning row).
Resume Rib for 1"/2.5cm.

Joining Row: Fold the knit section in half along turning
ridge so that purled row becomes top edge of piece. Join
working sts to CO edge as follows: *with left needle, pick
up the first st from the CO edge and knit tog with next
working st; rep from * to last 8 sts, knit to end of rnd.

Switch to larger needles. Knit one round.

Short-Row Shaping

Short Row 1: K14 (14, 15, 15, 16), W&T.

Short Row 2: P28 (28, 30, 30, 32), W&T.

Short Row 3: Knit to wrap, pick up wrap and knit together
with next st, k1, W&T.

Short Row 4: Purl to wrap, pick up wrap and purl together
with next st, p1, W&T.

Work Short Rows 3–4 a total of 6 times—56 (56, 58, 58, 60)
sts in between the wraps.

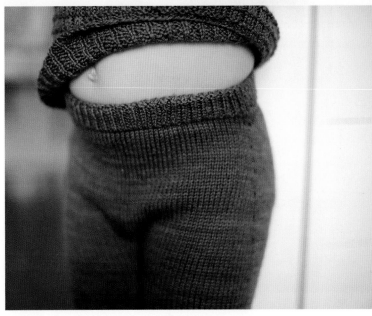

Resume knitting in the round, picking up rem wraps on
next round.

Next Rnd: K28 (29, 30, 31, 33), pm, k56 (58, 60, 62, 66), pm,
k to end of rnd.

Inc Rnd: [Knit to 1 st before marker, M1L, k1, sm, k1, M1R]
twice, k to end of rnd—4 sts inc.

Crotch Shaping

Set-up Rnd: K1, pm, k66 (68, 70, 72, 76), pm, k2, pm, k to last st, pm, k1.

Inc Rnd: [K to marker, M1R, sm, k to marker, sm, M1L] twice, k to end of rnd—4 sts inc.

Work Inc Rnd every other rnd a total of 5 times—156 (160, 164, 168, 176) sts.

SEPARATE FOR LEGS

Knit to 1 st before second marker, sl next 14 sts (removing markers) to scrap yarn for front of crotch, knit to 1 st before next marker, sl next 14 sts (removing markers) to scrap yarn for back of crotch, sl next 66 (68, 70, 72, 76) sts to holder for leg.

LEG (Make 2)

Note: Switch to DPNs when necessary.
Place marker and join to work in the round. Knit for 1"/2.5 cm.

Waffle Pattern

Rnds 1–3: *K1, p1, k1; rep from * around.
Rnd 4: Purl.
Set-up for Pattern: K0 (1, 1, 0, 1), work in Waffle Pattern to last 0 (1, 0, 0, 0) st, k to end of rnd.
Work Waffle Pattern twice as set.
Dec Rnd: K1, k2tog, work in Waffle Pattern as set to last 3 sts, ssk, k1—2 sts dec.
Continue working in Waffle Pattern, working Dec Rnd every 9 (10, 11, 12, 14) rnds a total of 14 times—38 (40, 42, 44, 48) sts. Work even in Waffle Pattern until inseam measures 17.5 (19.5, 21.5, 23.5, 25.5)"/44.5 (49.5, 54.5, 60, 65) cm from split with crotch.

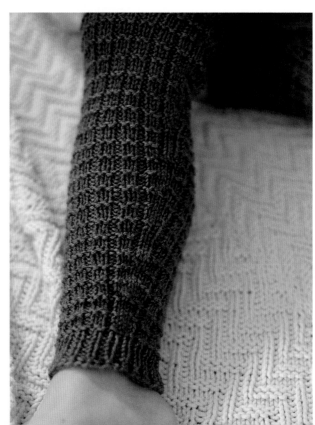

Work Inc Rnd on next rnd and every 7 rnds a total of 6 times—136 (140, 144, 148, 156) sts.
Remove side markers on next round.
Knit in the round until piece measures 6 (6.5, 7, 7.5, 8)"/15 (16.5, 18, 19, 20) cm from turning row at center front and then begin shaping for crotch.

Tucker
Military
Jacket

T his jacket boasts a double-breasted front and collar for warmth, as well as stitch detailing that will keep just enough of your brain involved while working the project. It features Grow-with-Me Tip #6, the turning ridge, which you can later let out for more length. Tucker is stylin' on the playground in the size 8.

Remove provisional CO from both shoulders and place 9 (10, 10, 10, 11) sts onto spare needles. With RS facing, [k1, p to last st, k1] across 7 (8, 8, 8, 9) left shoulder sts, pm, pick up and purl 6 (7, 7, 7, 9) sts along vertical edge, pm, [k1, p to end of row] provisionally cast on sts from left shoulder, cable cast on 13 (15, 17, 19, 19) sts, [p to last st, k1] across 9 (10, 10, 10, 11) provisionally cast on sts for right shoulder, pm, pick up and purl 6 (7, 7, 7, 9) sts along vertical edge, pm, [k1, p to last st, k1] 7 (8, 8, 8, 9) right shoulder sts—57 (65, 67, 69, 77) sts: 7 (8, 8, 8, 9) front sts, 6 (7, 7, 7, 9) sleeve sts, 31 (35, 37, 39, 41) back sts.

Size
Standard Size: 4 (6, 8, 10, 12)
Finished Chest (Buttoned): 26 (28, 30, 31.75, 34)"/66 (71, 76, 80.5, 86) cm

Gauge
14 sts and 19 rows in St st = 4"/10 cm square

Yarn
500 (560, 650, 750, 830) yd./457 (510, 600, 685, 760) m bulky weight #5 yarn (shown in Lorna's Laces Shepherd Bulky; 100% wool; 140 yd./128 m per 4 oz./114 g skein; Ascot)

Needles and Other Materials
- US 10 (6 mm) 24"/60 cm circular needle
- US 10 (6 mm) set of 5 double-pointed needles
- Stitch markers
- 8 (10, 10, 10, 12) 1"/2.5 cm buttons (ones shown are by Pollika)

Pattern Notes
- Jacket is worked top-down with seamless set-in sleeves.
- Button band is worked alongside sweater and overlaps in front for double breast.
- Collar is worked separately and seamlessly attached.

Body

RIGHT SHOULDER
Provisionally CO 9 (10, 10, 10, 11) sts.
Next Row (RS): K1, p to last st, k1.
Next Row (WS): P1, k to 3 sts from end, k2tog, p1.
Rep last 2 rows once more—7 (8, 8, 8, 9) sts.
Work back and forth in Rev St st with 1 st selvedge for 4 more rows, ending after a WS row. Break yarn.

LEFT SHOULDER
Provisionally CO 9 (10, 10, 10, 11) sts.
Next Row (RS): K1, p to last st, k1.
Next Row (WS): P1, ssk, k to last st, p1.
Rep last 2 rows once more—7 (8, 8, 8, 9) sts.
Work back and forth in Rev St st with 1 st selvedge for 4 more rows, ending after a WS row. Do not break yarn.

Next row (WS): P1, M1R, k to 1 st before marker, p1, sm, *p1, M1L, k to 1 st before marker, M1R, p1, sm, P1, k to one st before marker, p1, rep from * to next marker, sm, p1, knit to last st, M1L, p1—63 (71, 73, 75, 83) sts: 8 (9, 9, 9, 10) front sts, 8 (9, 9, 9, 11) sleeve sts, 31 (35, 37, 39, 41) back sts.

Work 1 row in pat, knitting the knit sts and purling the purls.

Next row (WS): *P1, k to 1 st before marker, p1, sm, p1, M1L, k to 1 st before marker, M1R, p1, sm, rep from * once more, k to end, cable CO 18 (19, 20, 20, 20) sts.

Next row: Sl 2 purlwise with yarn in back, K17 (18, 19, 19, 19), work in pat to end of row, CO 18 (19, 20, 20, 20) sts—103 (113, 117, 119, 127) sts: 26 (28, 29, 29, 30) front sts, 10 (11, 11, 11, 13) sleeve sts, 31 (35, 37, 39, 41) back sts.

Note: Sl the first 2 sts of every row purlwise, always holding yarn to WS.

Sleeve Inc Row (WS): Sl 2 purlwise with yarn in front, p17 (18, 19, 19, 19), *work to marker, sm, p1, M1R, k to 1 st before marker, M1L, p1, sm, rep from * once more, work in pat to end of row—4 sts inc.

Work Sleeve Inc Row a total of 4 (4, 4, 4, 3) times every RS row—119 (129, 133, 135, 139) sts: 26 (28, 29, 29, 30) front sts, 18 (19, 19, 19, 19) sleeve sts, 31 (35, 37, 39, 41) back sts.

Note: The following section contains work to be done at the same time. Read through section before beginning.

Buttonhole Row (RS): Sl 2, k3, work three-stitch buttonhole (see page 29), k3 (4, 5, 5, 5), work three-stitch buttonhole, work in pat to end of row.

Work Buttonhole Row on a RS row every 2.5 (2.25, 2.5, 3, 2.5)"/6.25 (5.75, 6.25, 7.5, 6.25) cm a total of 4 (5, 5, 5, 6) times and *at the same time* continue as directed.

Underarm Inc Row (WS): *Work to 1 st before marker, M1R, p1, sm, p1, M1L; rep from * 3 more times, work to end—8 sts inc.

Work Underarm Inc Row every WS row a total of 5 (5, 6, 7, 7) times—159 (169, 181, 191, 195) sts: 31 (33, 35, 36, 37) front sts, 28 (29, 31, 33, 33) sleeve sts, 41 (45, 49, 53, 55) back sts.

Work stitches as they appear, back and forth, until piece measures 5 (5.5, 6, 6.5, 7)"/12.5 (14, 15.25, 16.5, 17.75) cm from back neck CO edge, ending after a WS row.

SEPARATE BODY AND SLEEVES

Note: Remember to work Buttonhole Row on a RS row every 2.5 (2.25, 2.5, 3, 2.5)"/6.25 (5.75, 6.25, 7.5, 6.25) cm. Continue slipping the first 2 sts of every row.

Separation Row (RS): [Work to marker, sl 28 (29, 31, 33, 33) sleeve sts to hold, CO 4 (4, 4, 4, 6) sts] twice, work to end of row—111 (119, 127, 133, 141) sts.

Next Row: Sl 2, p17 (18, 19, 19, 19), k to last 21 sts, p21.

Work stitches as they appear until piece measures 13.25 (14.5, 16.5, 18, 19)"/33.5 (37, 42, 46, 48) cm from back neck CO edge, ending after a WS row and making sure all buttonhole rows have been worked before beginning hem.

HEM

Work back and forth in St st for 1"/2.5 cm.
Purl one RS row (turning ridge).
Work one more inch in St st.
BO all sts.
Fold to WS along turning ridge and seam.

Sleeve (Make 2)

Note: Two additional sts are picked up than were CO at under-arm to minimize holes. Make second sleeve same as first.

Place 28 (29, 31, 33, 33) sleeve sts on DPNs, ready to work. With spare DPN and RS facing, starting at center under-arm, pick up and knit 2 (2, 2, 2, 3) sts. K1, p to last st around sleeve sts, k1, pick up and knit 2 (2, 2, 2, 3) sts, place marker and join to work in the round—34 (35, 37, 39, 41) sts.

Next Rnd: P3, k2, k to last 5 sts, k2, p3.

Work in pat for 1"/2.5 cm.

Dec Rnd: P3, k1, ssk, work to last 6 sts, k2tog, p1, k3—2 sts dec.

Work Dec Rnd every 10 rnds a total of 5 times—24 (25, 27, 29, 31) sts.

Work in pat until sleeve measures 11.5 (11.75, 12.5, 13.75, 15.25)"/29 (30, 31.75, 35, 38.5) cm.

Knit in the round (St st) for 1"/2.5 cm. Purl 1 round (turning ridge). Knit in the round for 1"/2.5 cm more. BO all sts. Fold to WS along turning ridge and seam.

Finishing

COLLAR

CO 63 (71, 75, 77, 81) sts.

Work back and forth in St st for 1"/2.5 cm.

Purl one RS row (turning ridge).

Work 1"/2.5 cm more in St st.

Joining Row: Fold the knit section in half. Join working sts to cast on edge as follows: *with left needle, pick up the first st from the cast on edge and knit tog with next working st; rep from * to end of row.

NECKLINE

With RS facing, pick up and knit 18 (19, 20, 20, 20) sts along right front CO edge, 7 (9, 9, 9, 11) sts along vertical shoulder piece, 13 (15, 17, 19, 19) sts along back neck, 7 (9, 9, 9, 11) sts along left front shoulder and 18 (19, 20, 20, 20) sts along left front CO edge—63 (71, 75, 77, 81) sts.

Work a three-needle bind-off (see page 30) to join Neckline sts with Collar sts.

Attach buttons on right front opposite buttonholes. Weave in all loose ends. Block.

FINISHED MEASUREMENTS

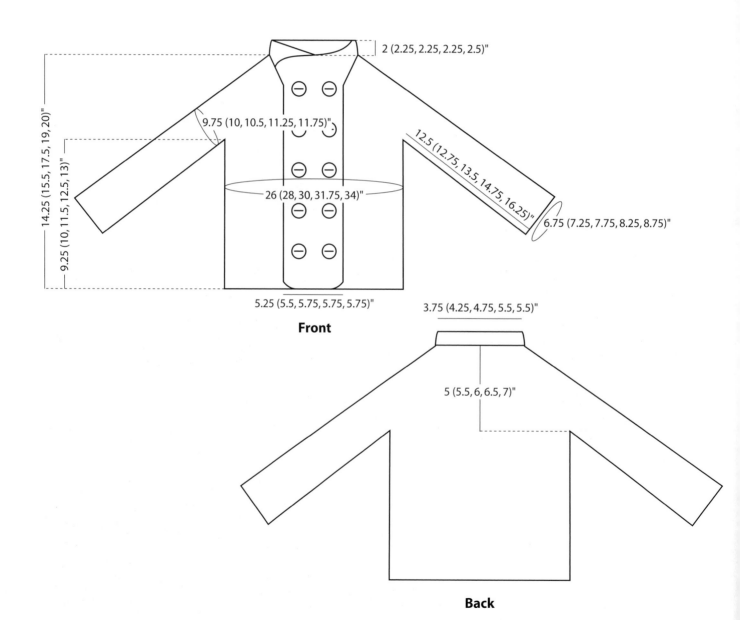

2 (2.25, 2.25, 2.25, 2.5)"

9.75 (10, 10.5, 11.25, 11.75)"

12.5 (12.75, 13.5, 14.75, 16.25)"

14.25 (15.5, 17.5, 19, 20)"

9.25 (10, 11.5, 12.5, 13)"

26 (28, 30, 31.75, 34)"

6.75 (7.25, 7.75, 8.25, 8.75)"

5.25 (5.5, 5.75, 5.75, 5.75)"

Front

3.75 (4.25, 4.75, 5.5, 5.5)"

5 (5.5, 6, 6.5, 7)"

Back

Touch-Me Texture

FROM RIBS TO COMPLEX CABLING, it is all included in this texture-rich section. Accessories, sweaters, vests, and even bottoms feature combinations of knits and purls that will entrance both knitter and recipient. You might just find yourself rereading the reference section in an effort to size it up for you.

Brothers'
Belt

Shown with Mattox Mittens and Hat

his funky, chunky accessory is stretchy and accommodating for growing boys. The cords are plaited and then knit back together for a three-dimensional texture. Charlie and Mattox are both sporting the size Medium.

Size

Standard Size: Small (Medium, Large)
Finished Length: 26 (28, 30)"/66 (71, 76) cm

Gauge

12-st garter tab measures approximately 2"/5 cm wide

Yarn

55 (60, 65) yd./50 (55, 60) m worsted weight #4 yarn (shown in Lorna's Laces Shepherd Worsted; 100% merino; 225 yd./206 m per 4 oz./114 g skein; Brick)

Needles and Other Materials

- US 6 (4 mm) double-pointed needles
- 4 safety pins
- Belt buckle

Belt

CO 4 sts.
Row 1: Knit.
Inc Row: K1, M1L, k to last st, M1R, k1.
Work last 2 rows twice—8 sts.
Knit 1 row.
Inc Row: K1, M1L, k2, M1L, k2, M1R, k2, M1R, k1—12 sts.
Sts will now be separated so that each cord can be worked separately.
Sl first 3 sts to RH needle. Sl next 3 sts to first safety pin, the foll 3 sts to a second pin, and the last 3 sts to a third pin. Sl sts on RH needle back to LH needle, ready to work.
Work I-cord (see page 28) over these 3 sts until cord measures 28 (30, 32)"/71 (76, 81) cm from garter tab. Sl these 3 sts to fourth safety pin. Break yarn.
Work separate I-cords on each set of 3 sts, breaking yarn at end and placing back on safety pin.
Four cords are secured with safety pins. Plait to end of cords.

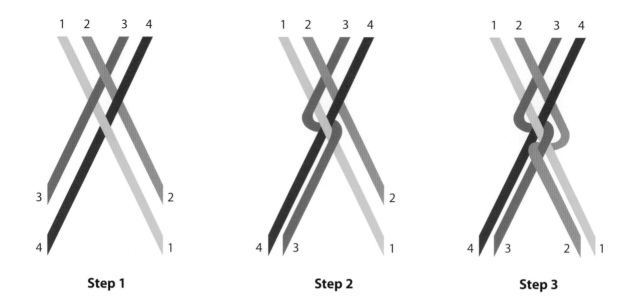

Step 1   **Step 2**   **Step 3**

Cords will not be exactly even due to pulling at different
   tensions. Once you have plaited to the bottom of the
   shortest cord, simply pull out some of the other cords to
   make them match if necessary.
Place all 12 sts, in order of finished plait position, back onto
   a single DPN and prepare to resume garter stitch.
Knit 1 row.
Dec Row: *K1, K2tog; rep from * to end of row—8 sts.
Knit every row in garter stitch for 1"/2.5 cm.
BO all sts, leaving a long tail for sewing.

Finishing

Wrap BO end around metal belt buckle, sew BO edge to
   Dec Row. Weave in all loose ends. Block.

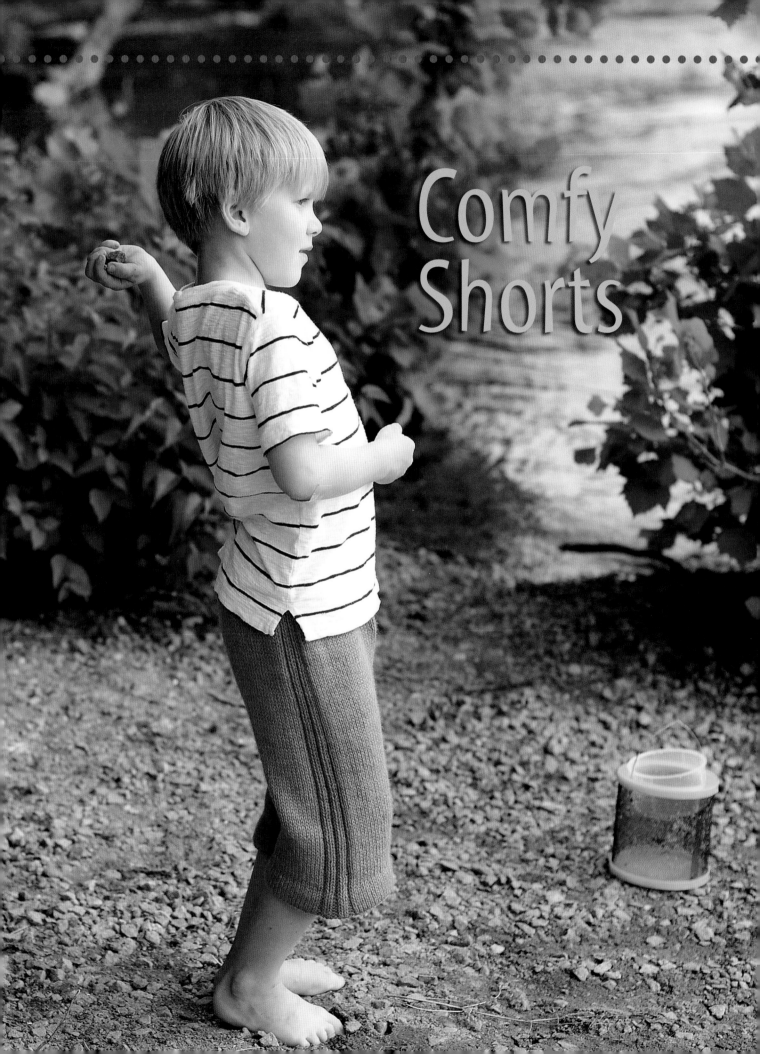

Comfy
Shorts

y boys are forever wanting to change into their "comfy shorts," which in the past has referred to a pair of gym or sweatshorts. This pattern was inspired by my desire to have them beg me to change into something that I knit for them instead. Jesse tested out the size Small shorts on the riverbank, and I'm happy to report that he did not want to take them off.

Size

Standard Size: Small (Medium, Large)
Finished Waist: 20 (22, 24)"/51 (56, 61) cm

Gauge

20 sts and 28 rows in St st on larger needles = 4"/10 cm
   square

Yarn

540 (710, 910) yd./500 (650, 830) m worsted weight #4 yarn
   (shown in Berroco Vintage; 50% acrylic, 40% wool, 10%
   nylon; 217 yd. /198 m per 3.5 oz./100 g skein; Caramel)

Needles and Other Materials

- US 6 (4 mm) 20"/50 cm circular needle
- US 7 (4.5 mm) 20"/50 cm circular needle
- 20 (22, 24)"/51 (56, 61) cm length of 1"/2.5 cm elastic

Waist and Hip

With smaller needles, CO 100 (110, 120) sts. Place marker
   and join to work in the round, being careful not to twist
   sts.
Rib: *K1, p1; rep from * around.
Work in Rib for 1.5"/3.75 cm.
Purl 1 row.
Resume Rib for 1.5"/3.75 cm.
Seaming Rnd: Fold the knit section in half along turning
   ridge so that purled row becomes bottom edge of piece.
   Join working sts to cast-on edge as follows: *with left
   needle, pick up the first st from the cast-on edge and knit
   tog with next working st; rep from * to last 4 sts, k4.
Switch to larger needles.
Inc Rnd: *K1, M1, k2, M1; rep from * to last 1 (2, 0) st, k to
   end of rnd—166 (182, 200) sts.

Short-Row Shaping

Short Row 1 (RS): K9 (10, 11), W&T.
Short Row 2 (WS): P17 (19, 22), W&T.
Short Row 3: K to wrap, pick up wrap and work tog with
   next st, k8 (9, 10), W&T.
Short Row 4: P to wrap, pick up wrap and work tog with
   next st, p8 (9, 10), W&T.

Work Short Rows 3–4 a total of 3 times (8 total short rows). Pick up rem wraps on next round. Knit to end of round.

Switch to larger needles.

Set-up for Leg Stripe: K37 (41, 45), p2, k2, p2, k2, p2, k73 (81, 90), p2, k2, p2, k2, p2, k to end of rnd.

Work in the round, in textured Leg Stripe Pattern until piece measures 10 (11, 12)"/25.5 (28, 30.5) cm from top edge of waistband (purled row).

Next Rnd: K1, pm, work 82 (90, 98) sts, pm, k1 (1, 2), pm, work to last 0 (0, 1) st, pm, k0 (0, 1)—1 (1, 2) sts in each crotch section.

Crotch Shaping Rnd: K1, [sm, M1R, work to marker, M1L, sm, work to marker] twice, work to end—4 sts inc.

Work Crotch Shaping Rnd EOR a total of 3 times—178 (194, 212) sts.

Work one round.

FINISHED MEASUREMENTS

Waist Circumference: 20 (22, 24)"

Hip Circumference: 33.25 (36.5, 40)"

Back Rise: 12.25 (13.25, 14.25)"

Front Rise: 11 (12, 13)"

Inseam: 7 (10, 13)"

Front

Separate Legs

Knit to first marker, removing marker, k1, sl last 9 (9, 10) sts to scrap yarn to place on hold for back crotch, work to 1 st before marker, sl next 9 (9, 10) sts to scrap yarn to place on hold for front crotch (removing markers), sl next 80 (88, 96) sts to hold for left leg—80 (88, 96) sts.

LEG (Make 2)

Join rem sts to work in the round, continuing striping down the side of leg, until leg measures 7 (10, 13)"/17.75 (25.5, 33) cm from split.

Purl one round.

Knit for 1"/2.5 cm. BO all sts, leaving a long tail for sewing.

Place rem 80 (88, 96) sts on needles and work left leg same as right.

Finishing

Graft front and back crotch sts together with Kitchener stitch (see page 28).

Sew 1"/2.5 cm hem of each pant leg to the WS, with purled round as bottom of leg.

Insert elastic inside waistband and sew length together. Use yarn tail to sew casing opening shut.

Block.

Triangles
Hat &
Scarf

can't count the number of times that my boys have come out of the house with clothing on inside out. This gear is completely reversible so that your kids won't have to think twice. The scarf features an opening so that it doesn't have to be double-wrapped around his neck to stay on. Bulky yarn creates lots of give, and therefore these one-size pieces keeping Tucker cozy will fit toddlers to young adults.

HAT

Size
Finished Circumference: 16.75"/42.5 cm

Gauge
10 sts and 15 rows in Triangles = 4"/10 cm square

Yarn
75 yd./70 m bulky weight #5 yarn (shown in Spud and Chloë Outer; 65% wool, 35% organic cotton; 60 yd./55 m per 3.5 oz./100 g skein; Bubble)

Needles and Other Materials
- US 11 (8 mm) 16"/40 cm circular needle
- US 11 (8 mm) set of 5 double-pointed needles
- Stitch marker

SCARF

Size
Finished Length: 50"/127 cm
Finished Width: 8"/20 cm

Gauge
10 sts and 15 rows in Triangles = 4"/10 cm square

Yarn
165 yd./150 m bulky weight #5 yarn (shown in Spud and Chloë Outer; 65% wool, 35% organic cotton; 60 yd./55 m per 3.5 oz./100 g skein; Bubble)

Needles and Other Materials
- US 11 (8 mm) 16"/40 cm circular needle
- US 11 (8 mm) set of 5 double-pointed needles
- Stitch marker

Hat

EAR FLAPS (Make 2)
Using 2 DPNs to work back and forth, CO 3 sts.
Purl 1 RS row.
Inc Row (WS): K1, M1L, k to last st, M1R—2 sts inc.
Work Inc Row every other row a total of 5 times—13 sts.
Set aside.

JOIN FLAPS WITH HAT
With circular needle, CO 3 sts, purl across 13 sts from first ear flap (RS facing), cable CO 10 sts, purl across 13 sts from second ear flap, CO 3 sts. Place marker and join to work in the round, being careful not to twist sts—42 sts.

Triangles (worked in the round)
Rnd 1: [K4, p1, k2, p1, k4, p2] 3 times.
Rnd 2: [K3, p2, k2, p2, k3, p2] 3 times.
Rnd 3: [K2, p3, k2, p3, k2, p2] 3 times.
Rnd 4: [K1, p4, k2, p4, k1, p2] 3 times.
Rnd 5: [P5, k2, p7] 3 times.
Rnd 6: Rep Rnd 4.

Triangles (worked in the round)
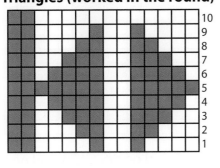

☐ Knit ▨ Purl

Rnd 7: Rep Rnd 3.
Rnd 8: Rep Rnd 2.
Rnd 9: Rep Rnd 1.
Rnd 10: [K12, p2] 3 times.
Rep 10 Rnds for pattern.
Work Triangles twice.
Work Rnds 1–6 once more.

CROWN SHAPING

Note: Switch to DPNs when necessary.
Rnd 1: [K2tog, p3, k2, p3, ssk, p2] 3 times—36 sts.
Rnd 2: [K2tog, p2, k2, p2, ssk, p2] 3 times—30 sts.
Rnd 3: [K2tog, p1, k2, p1, ssk, p2] 3 times—24 sts.
Rnd 4: [K2tog, k2, ssk, p2] 3 times—18 sts.
Rnd 5: [K2tog, ssk, p2] 3 times—12 sts.
Rnd 6: *P2tog; rep from * around—6 sts.
Break yarn, weave through remaining sts and secure.

Finishing

Use tails from ear flaps to sew up any gaps from joining round. Weave in all loose ends.

Scarf

CO 21 sts.

Triangles (worked back and forth)
Row 1: Sl 1, k3, p1, k4, p3, k4, p1, k4.
Row 2: Sl 1, p3, k2, p3, k3, p3, k2, p4.
Row 3: Sl 1, k3, p3, k2, p3, k2, p3, k4.
Row 4: Sl 1, p3, k4, p1, k3, p1, k4, p4.
Row 5: Sl 1, k3, p13, k4.
Row 6: Rep Row 4.
Row 7: Rep Row 3.
Row 8: Rep Row 2.
Row 9: Rep Row 1.
Row 10: Sl 1, p8, k3, p9.

Triangles (worked back and forth)

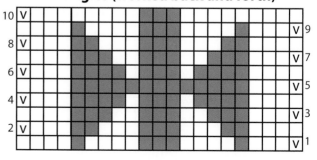

☐ Knit on RS, Purl on WS   ▨ Purl on RS, Knit on WS
Ⅴ Slip 1 st

Rep Rows 1–10 for pattern.

Work Triangles until scarf measures 35"/39 cm from CO
edge.

Next Row: Work 5 sts in pat, work 11-stitch buttonhole
(see page 29) over next 11 sts, work to end of row.

Resume Triangles until scarf measures 50"/127 cm from CO
edge, ending after a full repeat of pattern.

BO all sts.

Finishing

Weave in all loose ends. Block. Edges may roll slightly
depending on the fiber content of your yarn choice.

Mattox Hat &
Mittens

This stretchy stitch pattern lends itself to an extended fit. Extra length in the hat means it can be worn initially as a slouch and then later as a beanie for a growing head. The textured chevron is both modern and an easy pattern to memorize. Mattox is wearing the hat in Child size and the mittens in Small/Medium.

MITTENS

Size

Standard Size: Small/Medium (Medium/Large)
Finished Circumference: 7 (9.5)"/18 (24) cm

Gauge

18 sts and 24 rows in Chevron Pattern on larger needles = 4"/10 cm square

Yarn

125 (185) yd./115 (170) m worsted weight #4 yarn (shown in Spud and Chloë Sweater; 55% wool, 45% cotton; 160 yd./146 m per 3.5 oz./100 g skein; Beluga)

Needles and Other Materials

- US 6 (4 mm) set of 5 double-pointed needles
- US 7 (4.5 mm) set of 5 double-pointed needles
- Stitch marker

HAT

Size

Standard Size: Toddler (Child, Adult Small)
Finished Circumference: 17.75 (19.5, 21.25)"/45 (50, 54) cm

Gauge

18 sts and 24 rows in Chevron Pattern = 4"/10 cm square

Yarn

120 (140, 160) yd./110 (130, 150) m worsted weight #4 yarn (shown in Spud and Chloë Sweater; 55% wool, 45% cotton; 160 yd./146 m per 3.5 oz./100 g skein; Beluga)

Needles and Other Materials

- US 6 (4 mm) 16"/40 cm circular needle
- US 7 (4.5 mm) 16"/40 cm circular needle
- US 7 (4.5 mm) set of 5 double-pointed needles
- Stitch marker

Stitch Guide

Rib

*K1, p1; rep from * around.

Chevron Pattern

Rnds 1–2: *K5, p1, k1, p1; rep from * around.

Rnds 3–4: *P4, [k1, p1] twice; rep from * around.

Rnds 5–6: *K3, p1, k1, p1, k2; rep from * around.

Rnds 7–8: *P2, k1, p1, k1, p3; rep from * around.

Rnds 9–10: *K1, p1, k1, p1, k4; rep from * around.

Rnds 11–12: *K1, p1, k1, p5; rep from * around.

Rnds 13–14: *K1, p1, k5, p1; rep from * around.

Rnds 15–16: *K1, p5, k1, p1; rep from * around.

Chevron Pattern

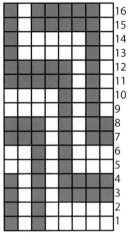

16
15
14
13
12
11
10
9
8
7
6
5
4
3
2
1

☐ Knit ■ Purl

Hat

With smaller circular needles, CO 80 (88, 96) sts. Place marker and join to work in the round, being careful not to twist stitches.

Work in Rib for 1"/2.5 cm. Switch to larger needles.

Work in Chevron Pattern until hat measures 6 (6.5, 7)"/15.25 (16.5, 18) cm from CO edge, ending after Rnd 2, 6, 10, or 14 of pattern.

Next Rnd: Remove marker. Work in pat to beginning of first full p5 segment of pattern (between 2–7 sts worked), place new marker for end of rnd.

CROWN SHAPING

Note: Switch to DPNs when necessary.

Rnd 1: *P5, k1, k2tog; rep from * around—70 (77, 84) sts.

Rnd 2: *P5, k2tog; rep from * around—60 (66, 72) sts.

Rnd 3: *K4, p1, k1; rep from * around.

Rnd 4: *K4, k2tog; rep from * around—50 (55, 60) sts.

Rnd 5: *P3, k2; rep from * around.

Rnd 6: *P3, k2tog; rep from * around—40 (44, 48) sts.

Rnd 7: *K2, p1, k1; rep from * around.

Rnd 8: *K2, k2tog; rep from * around—30 (33, 36) sts.

Rnd 9: *P1, k2; rep from * around.

Rnd 10: *P1, k2tog; rep from * around—20 (22, 24) sts.

Rnd 11: *K2tog; rep from * around—10 (11, 12) sts.

Break yarn, weave through remaining sts and secure.

Finishing

Weave in all loose ends.

Mitten (Make 2)

With smaller needles, CO 32 (40) sts. Place marker and join to work in the round, being careful not to twist stitches. Work in Rib for 1"/2.5 cm. Switch to larger needles. Work in Chevron Pattern until mitten measures 5 (6)"/ 13 (15) cm from CO edge.

SET-UP FOR THUMB

Left Hand Only

Work 4 sts in Chevron Pattern, do not break yarn but k5 (6) sts with a length of scrap yarn, sl these 5 (6) sts back to LH needle and resume Chevron Pattern with working yarn.

Right Hand Only

Work in Chevron Pattern to last 9 (10) sts, do not break yarn but k5 (6) sts with a length of scrap yarn, sl these 5 (6) sts back to LH needle and resume Chevron Pattern with working yarn to end of round.

HAND

Both Hands

Continue in Chevron Pattern until mitten measures 8 (9.5)"/20 (24) cm from CO edge, ending after Rnd 4, 8, or 12 of pattern.

Next Rnd: Remove marker. Knit to first purl stitch of pattern (between 1–5 sts worked), place new marker for end of rnd.

Decreases

Rnd 1: *P1, k1, p1, k3, k2tog; rep from * around—28 (35) sts.
Rnd 2: *P1, k1, p1, k2, k2tog; rep from * around—24 (30) sts.
Rnd 3: *P1, k1, p1, k1, k2tog; rep from * around—20 (25) sts.
Rnd 4: *P1, k1, p1, k2tog; rep from * around—16 (20) sts.
Rnd 5: *P1, k1, k2tog; rep from * around—12 (15) sts.
Rnd 6: *P1, k2tog; rep from * around—8 (10) sts.
Rnd 7: *K2tog; rep from * around—4 (5) sts.
Break yarn, weave through rem sts and secure.

THUMB

Place 5 (6) sts on bottom on single DPN, and 4 (5) sts on top on second DPN. Carefully pull out scrap yarn for thumb. Knit sts from bottom DPN. Use a free DPN to pick up and knit 2 sts in the gap between bottom and top needles, then knit sts from top DPN. Use another DPN to pick up and knit 2 sts on other gap. Place marker for end of round—13 (15) sts.
Knit 10 (12) rounds.

Decreases

Rnd 1: *K2, k2tog; rep from * to last 1 (3) sts, k to end of rnd—10 (12) sts.
Rnd 2: *K1, k2tog; rep from * to last 1 (0) sts, k to end of rnd—7 (8) sts.
Rnd 3: *K2tog; rep from * to last 1 (0) sts, k to end of rnd—4 sts.
Break yarn, weave through rem sts and secure.

Finishing

Weave in all loose ends.

Twisty Crew

This bulky sweater features funky twisted stitch columns from bottom to top. It's the perfect design for when you need to get a project completed quickly (thanks to the larger gauge). Kevin is getting creative in a size 10.

Size

Standard Size: 4 (6, 8, 10, 12)
Finished Chest: 25.25 (27.5, 29.75, 32, 33.25)"/64 (70, 75.5, 81, 84.5) cm

Gauge

14 sts and 19 rows in St st = 4"/10 cm square

Yarn

Bulky weight #5 yarn [shown in Plucky Knitter Plucky Bulky; 100% merino; 135 yd./123 m per 4 oz./113 g skein; Barn Door (A) and Dirty Martini (B)]
- Color A: 410 (460, 550, 640, 720) yd./375 (420, 500, 585, 660) m
- Color B: 70 (75, 80, 85, 95) yd./64 (70, 75, 80, 85) m

Needles and Other Materials

- US 11 (8 mm) 24"/60 cm circular needle
- US 11 (8 mm) set of 5 double-pointed needles
- Stitch markers

Pattern Notes

- This pattern is worked bottom-up with raglan-style seamless sleeves and a crew neck.
- The neckline is worked in an I-cord bind-off.

Stitch Guide

X2 (Crossover)

Knit into second st on LH needle, do not slide off needle.
Knit into first st on LH needle, slide both sts off needle.

Crossover Rib (worked over a multiple of 4 sts)

Rnd 1: *K2, p2; rep from * around.
Rnd 2: *X2, p2; rep from * around.
Repeat these 2 rnds for pattern.

Sleeve (Make 2)

With DPNs and B, CO 24 (24, 28, 28, 32) sts. Place marker and join to work in the round, being careful not to twist sts.
Work Crossover Rib twice. Switch to A. Knit 1 round.
Inc Rnd: *K1, M1L, k to last st, M1R, k1—2 sts inc.
Work Inc Rnd every 10 rnds a total of 4 (5, 4, 5, 5) times—32 (34, 36, 38, 42) sts.
Work even until sleeve measures 12.5 (12.75, 13.5, 14.75, 16.25)"/31.75 (32.25, 34.25, 37.5, 41.25) cm from CO edge.
Next Rnd: K to last 3 sts, sl next 6 sts to scrap yarn (removing marker) and place on hold for underarm—26 (28, 30, 32, 36) sts.
Break yarn and slip remaining sts to hold.

Body

Note: Create 4 bobbins of B after working hem. Carry yarn for A across columns of B as though stranding, but do not carry B, working from a separate bobbin at each column.

With circular needles and B, CO 88 (96, 104, 112, 116) sts. Place marker and join to work in the round, being careful not to twist sts. Work Crossover Rib twice.

Next Rnd: *With B, k2, with A, k6, with B, k2,** with A, k34 (38, 42, 46, 48), rep from * to **, with A, k to end of rnd.

Next Rnd: *With B, X2, with A, k6, with B, X2,** with A, k34 (38, 42, 46, 48), rep from * to **, with A, k to end of rnd.

Repeat last two rounds for body, working Crossover sts every other round in column. When body measures 9.5 (10, 11.5, 12.75, 13)"/24 (25.5, 29.25, 32.25, 33) cm from CO edge, join body and sleeves, ending after a Crossover Rnd.

JOINING BODY AND SLEEVES

Note: Continue working Crossover sts every other round and colorwork as set up for body throughout decrease sequence.

Joining Row: *With B, k2, sl next 6 sts to hold for underarm, with A, k26 (28, 30, 32, 36) sleeve sts, with B, k2,** with A, k34 (38, 42, 46, 48), rep from * to **, with A, k to end of rnd—128 (140, 152, 164, 176) sts: 34 (38, 42, 46, 48) back/front sts, 26 (28, 30, 32, 36) sleeve sts, 8 raglan sts.

Work 2 (4, 4, 4, 6) rounds in pattern.

Crossover Dec Rnd: [X2, k2tog, k to 2 sts before raglan column, ssk] 4 times—8 sts dec.

Work Crossover Dec Rnd EOR a total of 8 (8, 9, 10, 11) times—64 (76, 80, 84, 88) sts: 18 (22, 24, 26, 26) front/back sts, 10 (12, 12, 12, 14) sleeve sts, 8 raglan sts.

Next Rnd: Work in pat past second crossover column, k13 (15, 17, 19, 19) sts, sl last 8 (8, 10, 12, 12) sts to hold for front collar.

Sweater will now be worked back and forth.

Crossover Dec Row (RS): K1, ssk, [k to 2 sts before Crossover Column, ssk, X2, k2tog] 4 times, k to last 3 sts, k2tog, k1—10 sts dec.

Work Crossover Dec Row every RS row a total of 1 (2, 2, 2, 2) times—46 (48, 50, 52, 56) sts: 16 (18, 20, 22, 22) back sts, 3 front sts, 8 sleeve sts, 8 raglan sts.

Next Row (RS): K1, [ssk, X2, k2tog, k to 2 sts before Crossover Column] 3 times, ssk, X2, k2tog, k1—38 (40, 42, 44, 48) sts: 14 (16, 18, 20, 20) back sts, 2 front sts, 6 sleeve sts, 8 raglan sts.

Do not turn. Break yarn for A. Place front collar sts on spare DPN, ready to work.

With B, pick up and knit 3 (5, 5, 5, 5) sts along left front diagonal edge, knit across 8 (8, 10, 12, 12) front collar sts, pick up and knit 3 (5, 5, 5, 5) sts along right front diagonal edge, knit across 38 (40, 42, 44, 48) neckline sts—52 (58, 62, 66, 70) sts. Work I-cord bind-off (see page 28).

Finishing

Graft underarms closed with Kitchener stitch (see page 28). Weave in all loose ends. Block.

FINISHED MEASUREMENTS

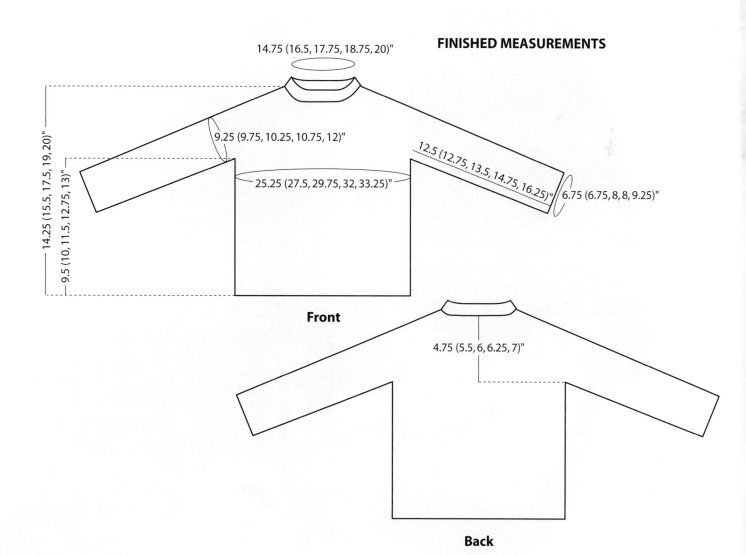

14.75 (16.5, 17.75, 18.75, 20)"

14.25 (15.5, 17.5, 19, 20)"

9.5 (10, 11.5, 12.75, 13)"

9.25 (9.75, 10.25, 10.75, 12)"

25.25 (27.5, 29.75, 32, 33.25)"

12.5 (12.75, 13.5, 14.75, 16.25)"

6.75 (6.75, 8, 8, 9.25)"

Front

4.75 (5.5, 6, 6.25, 7)"

Back

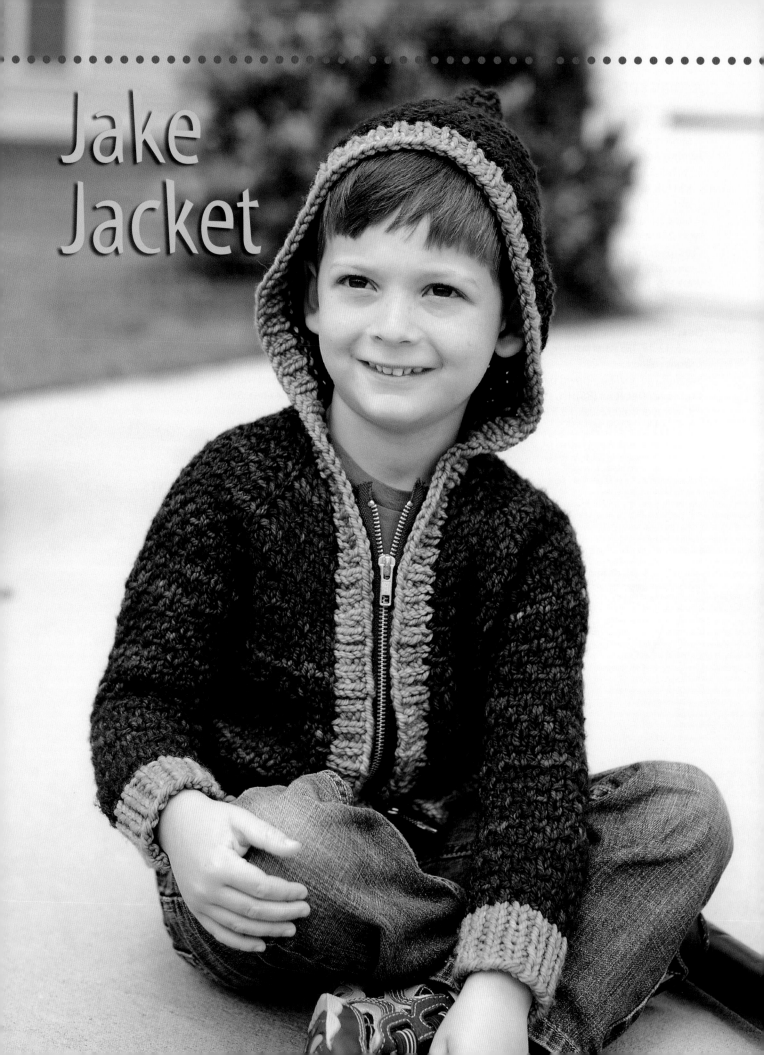

Jake Jacket

This layering piece has a looser stitch than some of the other sweaters, making it breathable though it's worked in a bulky weight yarn. Don't be afraid of the zipper—kids adore them and it makes your knitting so wearable. If you are feeling intimidated, review the instructions for an easy no-sew zipper on page 30. Jake played around in a size 4 and enjoyed filling his pockets with treasures.

Size

Standard Size: 4 (6, 8, 10, 12)
Finished Chest (zipped): 25.75 (27.75, 29.5, 32, 34.5)"/65.5
    (70.5, 75, 81, 87.5) cm

Gauge

13 sts and 19 rows in Slip Stitch Pattern on larger needles =
    4"/10 cm square

Yarn

Bulky weight #5 yarn [shown in Plucky Knitter Plucky Bulky;
    100% merino; 135 yd./123 m per 4 oz./113 g skein; Dirty
    Martini (A) and Iced Audrey (B)]
- Color A: 450 (500, 600, 690, 780) yd./410 (460, 550, 630,
    720) m
- Color B: 110 (115, 120, 130, 140) yd./100 (105, 110, 120,
    130) m

Needles and Other Materials

- US 10.5 (6.5 mm) 36"/90 cm circular needle
- US 10.5 (6.5 mm) set of 5 double-pointed needles
- US 11 (8 mm) 36"/90 cm circular needle
- US 11 (8mm) set of 5 double-pointed needles
- Stitch markers
- 13.25 (14.5, 16.5, 18, 19)"/33.5 (37, 42, 46, 48) cm two-way
    separating zipper

Pattern Notes

- This sweater is worked from the bottom up with vertical
    set-in pockets and raglan-style seamless sleeves.
- The hood is worked directly from the neckline and
    closed with a three-needle bind-off.

Stitch Guide

IN THE ROUND

Rib (worked over an even number of sts)

Rnd 1: *K1, p1; rep from * around.
Repeat this round for pattern.

Slip Stitch Patterned Increase

*Note: Hold yarn in front while slipping stitches. Slip stitches
    purlwise. 2 sts are increased after each pattern repeat.*
Rnd 1 and odd rnds: Knit.

Rnd 2: *K1, sl 1; rep from * around.
Rnd 4: *Sl 1, k1; rep from * around.
Rnd 5: K1, M1L, k to end of rnd.
Rnd 6: *Sl 1, k1; rep from * to last st, sl 1.
Rnd 8: *K1, sl 1; rep from * to last st, k1.
Rnd 10: Rep Rnd 6.
Rnd 12: Rep Rnd 8.
Rnd 13: Rep Rnd 5.
Rnd 14–16: Rep Rnds 2–4.
Repeat these 16 rounds for pattern.

BACK AND FORTH

Rib (worked over an odd number of sts)

Row 1 (WS): *P1, k1; rep from * to last st, p1.
Row 2: *K1, p1; rep from * to last st, k1.
Repeat these 2 rows for pattern.

Slip Stitch Pattern
(worked over an odd number of sts)

*Note: Hold yarn in back while slipping stitches. Slip stitches
    purlwise.*
Row 1 (RS): Knit.
Row 2: P1, *p1, sl 1; rep from * to end of row.
Row 3: Knit.
Row 4: P1, *sl 1, p1; rep from * to end of row.
Repeat these 4 rows for pattern.

Pocket Linings

With a larger DPN and B, CO 20 (20, 22, 22, 26) sts. With 2 DPNs, slip first stitch to one DPN and second stitch to second DPN. Continue so that alternating sts are on two DPNs. Place marker and join to work in the round. Knit in the round until piece measures 3 (3, 3.5, 3.5, 4)"/7.5 (7.5, 9, 9, 10) cm from CO edge. BO all sts, leaving a long tail for sewing.

Sleeve (Make 2)

With smaller DPNs and B, CO 26 (28, 30, 30, 32) sts. Place marker and join to work in the round, being careful not to twist sts.

Work in Rib for 8 rounds. Switch to larger needles and A. Knit 1 round.

Work Slip Stitch Patterned Increase a total of 2 (2, 2, 3, 3) times—4 (4, 4, 6, 6) sts inc; 30 (32, 34, 36, 38) sts.

Continue working Rnds 1–4 *only* of Slip Stitch Pattern until sleeve measures 12.5 (13, 14, 15, 16)"/31.75 (33, 35.5, 38, 40.5) cm from CO edge, ending after a knit round.

Next Rnd: Work in pat to last 2 (2, 3, 3, 3) sts, sl next 4 (4, 6, 6, 6) sts to scrap yarn (removing marker) and place on hold for underarm, noting which round of pattern was just completed—26 (28, 28, 30, 32) sts.

Break yarn and slip remaining sts to hold.

Body

With smaller circular needles and B, CO 75 (81, 87, 95, 103) sts. Work back and forth in Rib for 7 rows, ready to work a WS row. Switch to larger needles and A.

Work in Slip Stitch Pattern for 4 rows.

POCKET SHORT ROWS

Note: Openings for pockets are created by working three sets of short rows. Because the gap is desired, there is no wrap and turn during the short-row shaping.

Next Row: K13 (13, 15, 15, 17).

Work back and forth in Slip Stitch Pattern (including 1-st selvedge) over these stitches only for 3 (3, 3.5, 3.5, 4)"/7.5 (7.5, 9, 9, 10) cm, ending after a RS row. Break yarn.

Attach yarn to next 49 (55, 57, 65, 69) sts and work back and forth in Slip Stitch Pattern (including 1-st selvedge) over these stitches to match length of first set of short rows, ending after a RS row. Break yarn.

Attach yarn to remaining 13 (13, 15, 15, 17) sts and work back and forth in Slip Stitch Pattern (including 1-st selvedge) over these stitches to match length of previous short rows, ending after a RS row. *Do not break yarn.*

Next Row (WS): Work in pat across the set of short rows just completed, join second and first sets of short rows as you come to them by working across them in pat. All three short rows should now be rejoined as the body and ready to be worked in full.

Work back and forth in Slip Stitch Pattern until body measures 9.5 (10.25, 11.75, 12.5, 13)"/24 (26, 30, 31.75, 33) cm, ending after the WS row of pattern that matches with the final round completed on each sleeve.

JOINING BODY AND SLEEVES

Note: After the joining row, each section is separated by a raglan faux seam. This single stitch is worked in stockinette while the Slip Stitch Pattern continues seamlessly around it. Because the decreases are mirrored, the stitch pattern does not need to be adjusted after each raglan decrease row. Continue working in Slip Stitch Pattern throughout decreases.

Joining Row: K15 (17, 17, 19, 21) sts, *pm, k1, sl next 4 (4, 6, 6, 6) sts to hold for underarm, pm, k26 (28, 28, 30, 32) sts from sleeve, pm, k1, pm,** k33 (35, 37, 41, 45) sts, rep from * to **, k to end of row—119 (129, 131, 143, 155) sts: 33 (35, 37, 41, 45) back sts, 26 (28, 28, 30, 32) sleeve sts, 15 (17, 17, 19, 21) front sts, 4 raglan sts.

Next Row: [Work in Slip Stitch Pattern to marker, sm, p1, sm] 4 times, work in pattern to end of row.

Raglan Dec Row (RS): [K to 2 sts before marker, ssk, sm, k1, sm, k2tog] 4 times, k to end of row—8 sts dec.

Continue working in Slip Stitch Pattern with stockinette faux seam and *at the same time* work Raglan Dec Row every RS row a total of 9 (10, 10, 11, 12) times—47 (49, 51, 55, 59) sts: 15 (15, 17, 19, 21) back sts, 8 sleeve sts, 6 (7, 7, 8, 9) front sts, 4 raglan sts.

Next Row (WS): BO 3 (4, 4, 5, 6) sts, work in pat with faux seam to end of row.

Next Row: BO 3 (4, 4, 5, 6) sts, [k to 2 sts before marker, ssk, sm, k1, sm, k2tog] 4 times, k to end of row—33 (33, 35, 37, 39) sts: 13 (13, 15, 17, 19) back sts, 6 sleeve sts, 2 front sts, 4 raglan sts.

Work Raglan Dec Row once more on next RS row—25 (25, 27, 29, 31) sts: 11 (11, 13, 15, 17) back sts, 4 sleeve sts, 1 front st, 4 raglan sts.

Work one WS row in pat, removing all markers.

Hood

Note: After the set-up row, a center stitch creates a new faux seam. This single stitch is worked in stockinette while the Slip Stitch Pattern continues seamlessly around it. Because the increases are mirrored, the stitch pattern does not need to be adjusted after each increase row. Continue working in Slip Stitch Pattern throughout work for hood.

Set-up Row: K12 (12, 13, 14, 15) sts, pm, k1, pm, k to end of row.

Next Row: Work in pat to marker, sm, p1, sm, work in pat to end of row.

Inc Row (RS): K to marker, M1R, sm, k1, sm, M1L, k to end of row—2 sts inc.

Work Inc Row every RS row a total of 11 times—47 (47, 49, 51, 53) sts.

Work back and forth in pat until hood measures 11 (11, 11.5, 11.5, 12)"/28 (28, 29, 29, 30.5) cm from back neck, ending after a RS row.

Flip hood inside out and fold in half. Work a three-needle bind-off (see page 30) to last st, BO last st.

Finishing

ZIPPER BAND

With RS facing, smaller needles, and B, pick up and knit 4 sts for every 5 rows beginning at left front, continuing around entire hood and down right front, ending with an odd number of sts. Work back and forth in Rib for 3 rows. BO all sts.

POCKETS

With RS facing, smaller needles, and B, pick up and knit 11 (11, 13, 13, 15) sts on pocket opening on side closest to center front. Work back and forth in Rib for 3 rows. BO all sts, leaving a long tail for sewing. Use BO and CO tails to sew sides of ribbing to body of sweater. Attach pocket linings to the WS of sweater using tail from BO.

Attach zipper to sweater (see page 30). Graft underarms closed with Kitchener stitch (see page 28). Weave in all loose ends. Block.

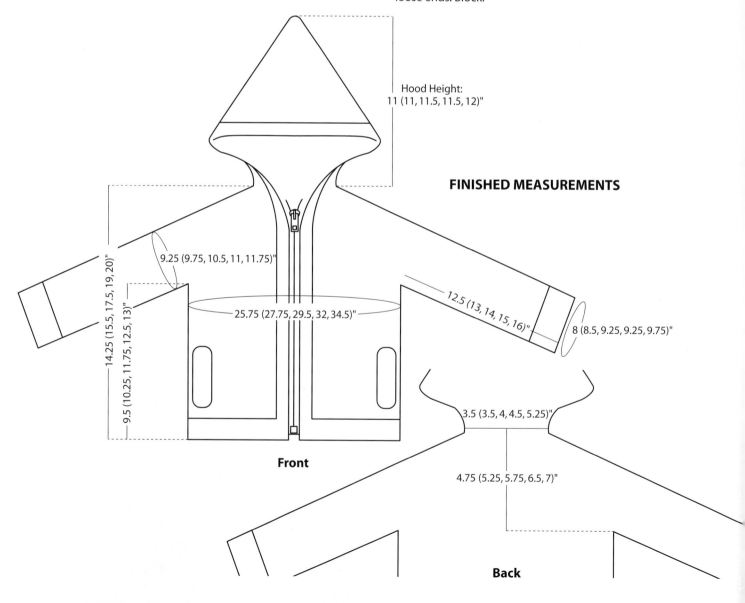

FINISHED MEASUREMENTS

Hood Height: 11 (11, 11.5, 11.5, 12)"

9.25 (9.75, 10.5, 11, 11.75)"

14.25 (15.5, 17.5, 19, 20)"

9.5 (10.25, 11.75, 12.5, 13)"

25.75 (27.75, 29.5, 32, 34.5)"

12.5 (13, 14, 15, 16)"

8 (8.5, 9.25, 9.25, 9.75)"

3.5 (3.5, 4, 4.5, 5.25)"

4.75 (5.25, 5.75, 6.5, 7)"

Front

Back

Jesse
Half-Zip

his toasty warm sweater features a double-sided collar and a half-zip placket to keep the appropriate amount of warmth in and the cold out. The easy-to-memorize cable repeat adds a textural sophistication for a true modern "little man" look. Jesse is wearing the size 8.

Size

Standard Size: 5 (8, 10, 12)
Finished Chest: 25 (27.75, 30.5, 33.5)"/63.5 (70.5, 77.5, 85) cm

Gauge

23 sts and 28 rows in Cable Pattern on larger needles = 4"/10 cm square

Yarn

700 (830, 975, 1100) yd./640 (760, 900, 1000) m worsted weight #4 yarn (shown in Anzula For Better or Worsted; 80% merino, 10% cashmere, 10% nylon; 200 yd./183 m per 4 oz./115 g skein; Toffee)

Needles and Other Materials

- US 7 (4.5 mm) 24"/60 cm circular needle
- US 7 (4.5 mm) set of 5 double-pointed needles
- Stitch markers
- 7.5"/19 cm zipper

Pattern Notes

- Cable work in this pattern is both written and charted; use whichever notation is more comfortable for you. The same chart is used when working in the round or back and forth; work even-numbered rows from left to right when working flat.
- This sweater is worked bottom-up, in the round, with raglan-style seamless sleeves.
- The collar is worked separately and grafted to the completed sweater.

Stitch Guide

T4B

Slip 2 sts to cable needle and hold to back, k2, p2 from cable needle.

T4F

Slip 2 sts to cable needle and hold to front, p2, k2 from cable needle.

X2 (Crossover)

Knit into second st on LH needle, do not slide off needle. Knit into the first st on LH needle, slide both sts off needle.

Crossover Rib

All odd rnds: *K2, p2; rep from * around.
Rnd 2: *X2, p2, k2, p2; rep from * around.
Rnd 4: *K2, p2, X2, p2; rep from * around.
Rnd 6: *X2, p2, k2, p2; rep from * around.
Rnd 8: *K2, p2, X2, p2; rep from * around.
Work one more round in Rib.

Diamond Cables (worked in the round over 16 sts)

Rnd 1: *K1, p3, T4B, T4F, p3, k1; rep from * around.
Rnd 2: *K1, p3, k2, p4, k2, p3, k1; rep from * around.
Rnd 3: *K1, p1, T4B, p4, T4F, p1, k1; rep from * around.
Rnd 4: *K1, p1, k2, p8, k2, p1, k1; rep from * around.
Rnd 5: *K1, p1, T4F, p4, T4B, p1, k1; rep from * around.
Rnd 6: *K1, p3, k2, p4, k2, p3, k1; rep from * around.

Diamond Cables

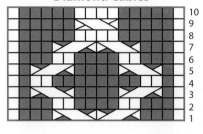

- ☐ 16-st repeat
- ☐ Knit on RS, Purl on WS
- ■ Purl on RS, Knit on WS

- ⬜ C4F
- ⬜ T4B
- ⬜ T4F

Rnd 7: *K1, p3, T4F, T4B, p3, k1; rep from * around.
Rnd 8: *K1, p5, k4, p5, k1; rep from * around.
Rnd 9: *K1, p5, C4F, p5, k1; rep from * around.
Rnd 10: *K1, p5, k4, p5, k1; rep from * around.
Rep 10 rounds for pattern.

Diamond Cables
(worked back and forth over 16 sts)

Row 1 (RS): *K1, p3, T4B, T4F, p3, k1; rep from * to end of row.
Row 2: *P1, k3, p2, k4, p2, k3, p1; rep from * to end of row.
Row 3: *K1, p1, T4B, p4, T4F, p1, k1; rep from * to end of row.
Row 4: *P1, k1, p2, k8, p2, k1, p1; rep from * to end of row.
Row 5: *K1, p1, T4F, p4, T4B, p1, k1; rep from * to end of row.
Row 6: *P1, k3, p2, k4, p2, k3, p1; rep from * to end of row.
Row 7: *K1, p3, T4F, T4B, p3, k1; rep from * to end of row.
Row 8: *P1, k5, p4, k5, p1; rep from * to end of row.
Row 9: *K1, p5, C4F, p5, k1; rep from * to end of row.
Row 10: *P1, k5, p4, k5, p1; rep from * to end of row.
Rep 10 rows for pattern.

Body

With circular needles, CO 144 (160, 176, 192) sts. Place marker and join to work in the round, being careful not to twist sts.
Work 9 rnds of Crossover Rib.
Next Rnd: Work in Diamond Cables.

Work in the round, repeating Diamond Cables until piece measures 9.75 (10.75, 11.75, 12)"/24.75 (27, 30, 30.5) cm, ending after an odd-numbered round.

Sleeve (Make 2)

With DPNs, CO 36 (40, 44, 48) sts. Place marker and join to work in the round, being careful not to twist sts. Work 9-round Crossover Rib as for hem.
Next Rnd: K2, pm, p8 (10, 12, 14), pm, work Diamond Cables *once*, pm, p8 (10, 12, 14), pm, k2.
Inc Rnd: K to marker, M1L, sm, p to marker, sm, work Diamond Cables *once*, sm, p to marker, sm, M1R, k to end of rnd—2 sts inc.
Work in pat as established, adjusting increased sts to knit sts on the following round (your knit panel will get wider).
Work Inc Rnd every 6 (7, 7, 8) rnds a total of 10 times—56 (60, 64, 68) sts.
Work even in pat until sleeve measures 12 (13, 14.5, 15.5)"/30.5 (33, 37, 39) cm from CO edge, ending one round prior to the last round of Diamond Cables worked on body.
Next Rnd: Work to last 3 (3, 4, 4) sts, sl next 6 (6, 8, 8) sts to hold for underarm—50 (54, 56, 60) sts.

Join Body and Sleeves

Note: Continue working in Diamond Cables on body and sleeves as established. Round marker will be at center front. Allow cables to naturally disappear once the stitches become part of the raglan decreases. Decrease Rounds should line up with odd-numbered chart rounds.
Joining Rnd: Work 32 (36, 39, 43) sts, *pm, k1, pm, sl next 6 (6, 8, 8) sts to hold for underarm, work 50 (54, 56, 60) sts from sleeve, pm, k1, pm,** work 64 (72, 78, 86) back sts, rep from * to **, work to end of rnd—232 (256, 272, 296) sts: 64 (72, 78, 86) front/back sts, 50 (54, 56, 60) sleeve sts, 4 raglan sts.
Dec Rnd: [Work to 2 sts before marker, ssk, sm, k1, sm, k2tog] 4 times, work to end of rnd—8 sts dec.

Work Dec Rnd every other rnd a total of 8 (10, 11, 14) times—168 (176, 184, 184) sts: 48 (52, 56, 58) front/back sts, 34 (34, 34, 32) sleeve sts, 4 raglan sts.

Work one round.

Sweater will now be worked back and forth to form the placket.

Dec Row (RS): Sl 1, k1, [work to 2 sts before marker, ssk, sm, k1, sm, k2tog] 4 times, work to last 2 sts, k2—8 sts dec.

Next Row (WS): Sl 1, p1, work in pat to last 2 sts, p2.

Work Dec Row every RS row a total of 13 times—64 (72, 80, 80) sts: 22 (26, 30, 32) back sts, 11 (13, 15, 16) front sts, 8 (8, 8, 6) sleeve sts, 4 raglan sts.

Place sts on hold.

Collar

CO 64 (72, 80, 80) sts.

Rib

Row 1 (WS): P1, *k2, p2; rep from * to last 3 sts, k2, p1.

Row 2: K1, *p2, k2; rep from * to last 3 sts, p2, k1.

Repeat these last two rows until piece measures 3"/7.5 cm from CO edge, ending after a WS row.

Turning Ridge: Purl 1 RS row.

Resume Rib until piece measures 3"/7.5 cm from purled row, ending after a WS row.

Seaming Row: BO 3 sts. Fold the ribbed section in half along turning ridge so that purled row becomes bottom edge of piece. Join working sts to cast-on edge as follows: *with left needle, pick up the fourth st from the cast-on edge and knit tog with next working st; rep from * to last 3 sts. BO 3 sts. Break yarn and set aside.

Join collar to neckline sts using three-needle bind-off (see page 30) as follows: Hold collar and neckline together with RS facing each other. With WS facing, work three-needle bind-off with collar and neckline sts.

Finishing

Graft underarm sts with Kitchener stitch (see page 28). Insert zipper (see page 30). Weave in all loose ends. Block.

FINISHED MEASUREMENTS

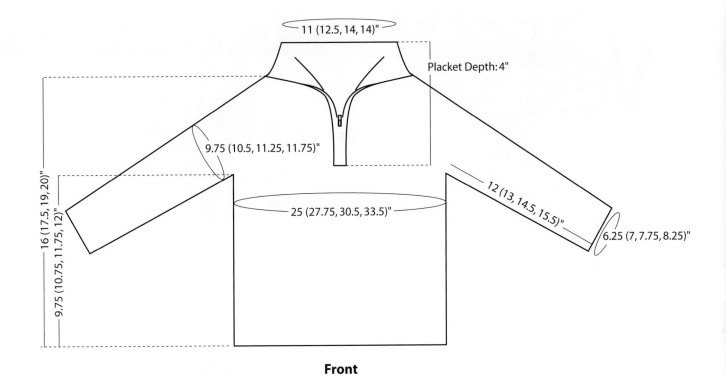

11 (12.5, 14, 14)"

Placket Depth: 4"

9.75 (10.5, 11.25, 11.75)"

16 (17.5, 19, 20)"

9.75 (10.75, 11.75, 12)"

25 (27.75, 30.5, 33.5)"

12 (13, 14.5, 15.5)"

6.25 (7, 7.75, 8.25)"

Front

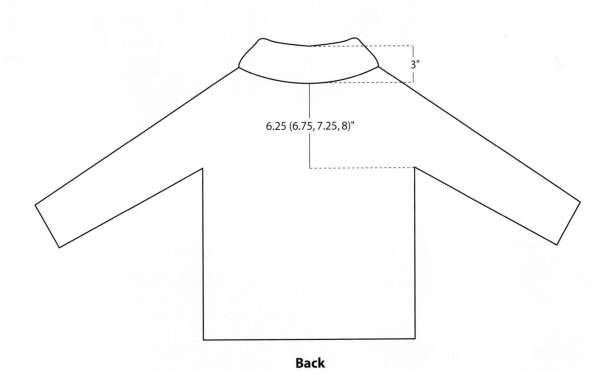

3"

6.25 (6.75, 7.25, 8)"

Back

Prepster
Vest

abling is my personal favorite technique. I love touching the fabric and watching the pattern emerge as it progresses. Cabling is paired with fingering weight yarn in this design. It's light and squishy and won't be too hot during transitional weather or light winters despite its Aran appearance. Jesse and Mattox (page 67) are both wearing the size 6. The wide wale rib on the back of the vest gives the knitter a break from cabling and also provides lots of stretch for growing.

Size

Standard Size: 4 (6, 8, 10, 12)
Finished Chest: 25 (27.25, 28.75, 31, 33)"/63.5 (69, 73, 78.75, 84) cm

Gauge

28 sts and 38 rows in Wide Wale Rib Pattern on larger needles = 4"/10 cm square
32 sts and 38 rows in Cable Pattern on larger needles = 4"/10 cm square

Yarn

400 (500, 575, 630, 750) yd./365 (460, 525, 575, 685) m fingering weight #1 yarn (shown in Anzula Squishy; 80% merino, 10% cashmere, 10% nylon; 375 yd./343 m per 4 oz./115 g skein; Denim)

Needles and Other Materials

- US 2 (2.75 mm) 24"/60 cm circular needle
- US 3 (3.25 mm) 24"/60 cm circular needle
- Stitch markers

Pattern Notes

- This pattern is geared toward experienced knitters. To complete it, you should be comfortable working with multiple charts and doing work *at the same time.*
- The vest is worked from the bottom up, in the round, until the armholes, and is completed back and forth.

Body

With smaller circular needles, CO 188 (204, 216, 232, 248) sts. Place marker and join to work in the round, being careful not to twist sts.
Rib: P1 (1, 0, 0, 0), *k2, p2; rep from * to last 3 (3, 0, 0, 0) sts, k2 (2, 0, 0, 0), p1 (1, 0, 0, 0).
Work in Rib for 1"/2.5 cm. Switch to larger needles.
During next round, begin chart work as noted beginning on Row 22 (2, 24, 16, 2) of Charts.
Next Rnd: P1 (1, 4, 4, 4), [K6, p2] 10 (11, 11, 12, 13) times, k6, p1 (1, 4, 4, 4), pm, p3 (5, 7, 9, 12), work Chart A, p1 (3, 4, 6, 7), work Chart B, p1 (3, 4, 6, 7), work Chart A, p3 (5, 7, 9, 12)—

88 (96, 102, 110, 118) back sts, 100 (108, 114, 122, 130) front sts.
Work in pat to end of charts, then work a total of 1 (1, 2, 2, 2) full chart repeats, then continue through Row 22 (20, 16, 10, 6) of charts, with wide wale rib at back and working charts across front. Piece should measure approximately 8.75 (10.75, 11.5, 11.75, 13)"/22 (27, 29, 30, 33) cm from CO edge. Place 88 (96, 102, 110, 118) sts for back on hold.

FRONT

Note: The next section includes work to be done at the same time. *Be sure to read through entire section before beginning.*

Work back and forth over 100 (108, 114, 122, 130) sts in Cable and Wide Wale Rib patterns as established, ready to work Row 23 (21, 17, 11, 7).

BO 7 (8, 9, 10, 11) sts at beg of next 2 rows, working charts over remaining sts—86 (92, 96, 102, 108) sts. The two outside cables will disappear during the decreasing.

Dec Row (RS): K1, ssk, work in pat to last 3 sts, k2tog, k1—2 sts dec.

Work Dec Row every RS row a total of 3 (4, 5, 6, 7) times—80 (84, 86, 90, 94) sts.

Next Row: K2, p1, work 74 (78, 80, 84, 88) sts in pat, p1, k2. Work even to end of chart repeat.

Next Row: K2, p1, work Chart C, p1 (3, 4, 6, 7), work Chart D, p1 (3, 4, 6, 7), work Chart E, p1, k2.

Work each of these Charts once with Rev St st background and selvedge sts as set-up in last row and *at the same time*, during last row, separate right and left front at center of Chart D by joining a second ball of yarn.

CHART A

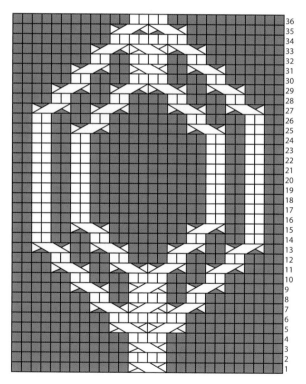

CHART B

☐ Knit on RS or when working in the round, Purl on WS

▨ Purl on RS or when working in the round, Knit on WS

◣◤ T4F: Sl 2 sts to CN and hold to front, p2, k2 from CN

◥◢ T4B: Sl 2 sts to CN and hold to back, k2, p2 from CN

◥◢ C4B: Sl 2 sts to CN and hold to back, k2, k2 from CN

◣◤ C4F: Sl 2 sts to CN and hold to front, k2, k2 from CN

◹ K2tog on RS or p2tog on WS

◺ SSK on RS or p2tog on WS

Right Front Neckline Shaping

Row 1 (WS): P2, k to last 13 sts, p2, k4, p2, k2, p2tog, p1.
Row 2: K1, ssk, p1, T4F, p2, T4F, p to last 2 sts, k1.

Left Front Neckline Shaping

Row 1 (WS): P1, p2tog, k2, p2, k4, p2, k to last 2 sts, p2.
Row 2: K1, p to last 14 sts, T4B, p2, T4B, p1, k2tog, k1.
Work Right Front and Left Front Neckline Shaping a total of 14 (13, 13, 13, 13) times. Work Row 1 once more—14 (16, 17, 19, 21) sts. Place sts on spare DPNs and set aside.

BACK

Place 88 (96, 102, 110, 118) sts for back on needle, ready to work RS back and forth.
Continue working sts as they appear throughout.

BO 7 (8, 9, 10, 11) sts at beg of next 2 rows—74 (80, 84, 90, 96) sts.
Dec Row (RS): K1, ssk, work in pat to last 3 sts, k2tog, k1—2 sts dec.
Work Dec Row every RS row a total of 7 (8, 9, 10, 11) times—60 (64, 66, 70, 74) sts.

CHART E

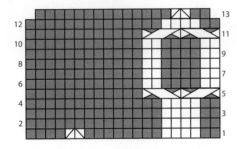

CHART C

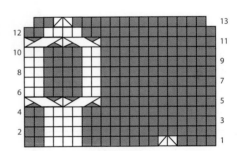

CHART D

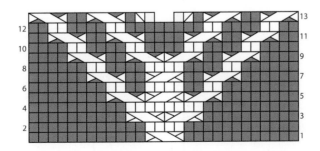

☐ Knit on RS or when working in the round, Purl on WS

■ Purl on RS or when working in the round, Knit on WS

T4F: Sl 2 sts to CN and hold to front, p2, k2 from CN

T4B: Sl 2 sts to CN and hold to back, k2, p2 from CN

C4B: Sl 2 sts to CN and hold to back, k2, k2 from CN

C4F: Sl 2 sts to CN and hold to front, k2, k2 from CN

☑ K2tog on RS or p2tog on WS

☒ SSK on RS or p2tog on WS

Work back and forth until back length matches front.
Flip piece inside out, holding RS together, three-needle BO
14 (16, 17, 19, 21) sts at shoulder together, BO 32 back
neck sts in pat with Jeny's Surprisingly Stretchy BO, three-
needle BO 14 (16, 17, 19, 21) sts at shoulder.

Finishing

ARMBANDS

With smaller needles, pick up and knit 88 (92, 100,
108, 116) sts along each armhole.
Rib: *K2, p2; rep from * around.
Work in Rib for 6 rounds. BO all sts.
Use tails at center front to tighten up any holes that
may have appeared during knitting. Weave in all
loose ends. Block.

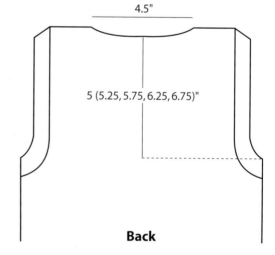

FINISHED MEASUREMENTS

Front

Back

Color Collection

THIS PLAYFUL SELECTION includes unexpected color combinations, graphics, and mix-and-match Fair Isle. You'll learn new techniques like intarsia "in the round" and perhaps gain confidence from the feedback you'll get when your little man sees what you are up to.

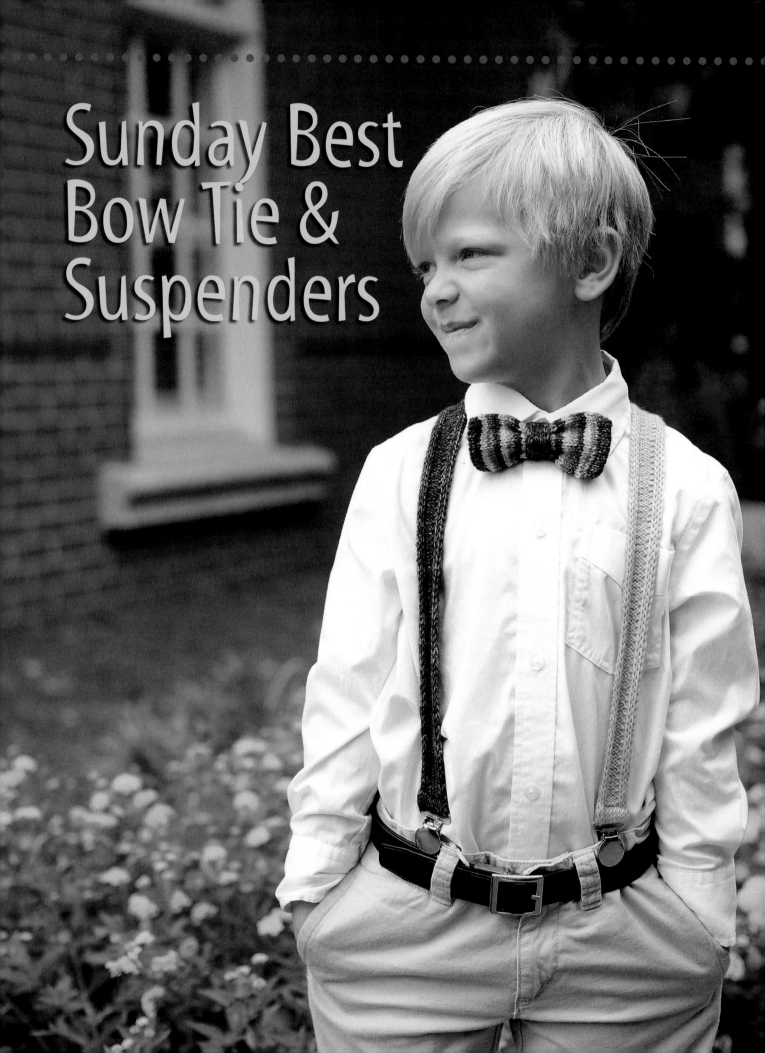

Sunday Best
Bow Tie &
Suspenders

Rib: *K1, p1; rep from * around.
Work in Rib for 1"/2.5 cm.
BO with Jeny's Surprisingly Stretchy BO (see page 28).
Repeat for second leg.

Finishing

Graft crotch closed with Kitchener stitch (see page 28).
Insert elastic at waistband and seam the two ends
together. Sew closed the opening on knit waistband.
Weave in ends. Block.

FINISHED MEASUREMENTS

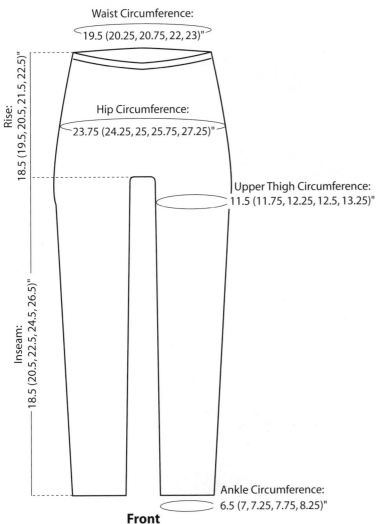

Waist Circumference:
19.5 (20.25, 20.75, 22, 23)"

Hip Circumference:
23.75 (24.25, 25, 25.75, 27.25)"

Upper Thigh Circumference:
11.5 (11.75, 12.25, 12.5, 13.25)"

Rise: 18.5 (19.5, 20.5, 21.5, 22.5)"

Inseam: 18.5 (20.5, 22.5, 24.5, 26.5)"

Ankle Circumference:
6.5 (7, 7.25, 7.75, 8.25)"

Front

ightweight accessories are a great way to spruce up a wardrobe even when the weather isn't calling for sweaters. Work these pieces in as many or as few colors as you like. Consider making the largest size suspenders and looping the extra length up and seaming it to the wrong side of each strap so that you can continue adjusting the length as he grows taller. Charlie is wearing the size Small.

SUSPENDERS

Size

Standard Size: Small (Medium, Large)
Finished Length: 22 (26, 30)"/56 (66, 76) cm

Gauge

Each 10-st strap measures approximately 1"/2.5 cm wide

Yarn

10 (12, 15) yd./25 (30.5, 38) m each Colors A and B and 5 yd./13 m Color C fingering #1 to DK #3 weight yarn

Needles and Other Materials

- US 3 (3.25 mm) needles
- Awl or leather hole punch
- Small scrap of leather for crossback
- Leather thread
- 3 metal suspender clips

BOW TIE

Size

Finished Width: 4"/10 cm
Finished Height: 2"/5 cm

Gauge

32 sts and 42 rows in St st = 4"/10 cm square

Yarn

Sport weight #2 or DK weight #3 yarn
- Color A: 30 yd./27 m
- Colors B and C: 10 yd./9 m each
(Multi-colored tie shown in Anzula Cricket; 80% merino, 10% nylon, 10% cashmere; 250 yd./229 m per 4 oz./114 g skein; Navy, Claret, and Daffodil.
Solid tie shown in Zitron Unisono; 100% merino; 328 yd./300 m per 3.5 oz./100 g skein; Canary.)

Needles and Other Materials

- US 3 (3.25 mm) set of 5 double-pointed needles
- Stitch marker
- Snap

Suspenders

Note: Colors are not noted in instructions. Work each strap in the color of your choice. Slipping stitches at the beginning of each row creates an I-cord edging effect without having to pick up stitches. Slip all sts purlwise. If you'd like to make length adjustments to the straps specific to your child, make the back strap one-third the length of the two longer straps to preserve the proportions.

STRAP (Make 3 Total: 2 Front and 1 Back)

CO 10 sts, leaving a long tail for sewing.
Slip the first 3 sts of every row.
Work back and forth in St st for 1"/2.5 cm, ending after a WS row.
Next Row (RS): Sl 3, p4, k3.
Next Row: Sl 3, k4, p3.
Repeat last two rows until strap measures either 18 (21, 24)"/46 (53, 61) cm for front straps, or 6 (7, 8)"/15 (18, 20) cm for back strap from CO edge. BO all sts.

Finishing

Leather Crossback

Trace template onto a separate piece of paper and cut it out. Use it to cut out your leather crossback piece. Do not cut out the circles inside the oval. Holding oval in line on top of cut out leather patch, use leather tool (either awl or punch) to create holes around perimeter of patch where indicated. You can punch through the paper and the leather simultaneously. With leather thread, sew BO ends of each strap to leather crossback piece.

Crossback Piece Template

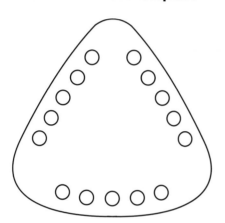

Insert CO ends of straps into suspender clips one at a time and stitch CO end to WS of strap. Make sure that the RS of strap corresponds with RS of clip when laid flat.

Weave in all loose ends. Steam block straps only; avoid getting leather crossback piece wet if possible.

Bow Tie

With A and a single DPN, CO 24 sts. With 2 DPNs, *sl 1 st to first DPN and next st to second DPN; rep from * until all sts are divided evenly onto two DPNs. Place marker and join to work in the round.

Next Rnd: K12, pm, k to end.

Inc Rnd: *K1, M1R, k to one st before marker, M1L, k1; rep from * once more—28 sts.

Knit one round. Work Inc Rnd once more—32 sts.

Stripes

Rnds 1–2: Knit in B.

Rnds 3–4: Knit in C.

Rnds 5–6: Knit in A.

Work in Stripes until bow tie measures 4"/10 cm from CO edge, ending after Rnd 4 of pattern. Break yarn for B and C; continue knitting in A.

Dec Rnd: *K1, k2tog, k to 3 sts before marker, ssk, k1; rep from * once more—28 sts.

Knit 1 round.

Work Dec Rnd once more—24 sts.

Flip piece inside out and weave in tails from B and C into the inside of the tie. Flip piece right side out. Arrange sts so that the first 12 sts are on one DPN and the second 12 sts are on another. Graft using Kitchener stitch (see page 28).

KNOT

With A, CO 7 sts. Sl first st of every row. Work back and forth in St st until piece measures 2.5"/6 cm from CO edge. BO all sts. Break yarn, leaving a long tail for sewing.

NECK BAND

With A, CO 7 sts. Sl first st of every row. Work back and forth in St st until piece measures 15"/38 cm from CO edge. BO all sts. Feel free to adjust this length to suit your recipient, or you can adjust the snap placement for a perfect and adjustable fit.

Finishing

Squeeze the middle of the bow tie and tightly wrap knot strip around it. Seam knot BO and CO ends together. Weave neck band through knot. Sew snap to neck band ends. Weave in all loose ends.

Stripy Socks

harlie's classic socks are worked toe-up with a contrasting toe and heel, then finished with simple stripy colorwork in the calf-length leg. This is a basic sock pattern you can work time and again with color modifications to keep you invested and your changing boy's interest piqued. Worn here in Child size.

Size

Standard Size: Toddler (Child, Teen)
Foot Circumference: 4.5 (5.75, 6.75)"/11.5 (14.5, 17) cm
Foot Length: 6 (7, 8)"/15.25 (17.75, 20.25) cm

Gauge

28 sts and 30 rows in St st = 4"/10 cm square

Yarn

Fingering weight #1 yarn [shown in Spud & Chloë Fine; 80% superwash wool, 20% silk; 248 yd./227 m per 2.3 oz./65 g skein; Snorkel (A), Sidewalk (B), and Calypso (C)]

- Color A: 80 (125, 185) yd./73 (115, 170) m
- Color B: 30 (45, 60) yd./30 (40, 55) m
- Color C: 20 (25, 30) yd./20 (25, 30) m

Needles and Other Materials

- US 2 (2.75 mm) set of 5 double-pointed needles
- US 3 (3.25 mm) set of 5 double-pointed needles
- US D-3 (3.25 mm) crochet hook
- Stitch markers

Pattern Notes

- Circumference is stretchy and sized with negative ease; measurement should be smaller than recipient.

Short Row Toe

With scrap yarn and crochet hook, provisionally CO 16 (20, 24) sts to larger DPN. With B, purl 1 WS row.

Short Rows 1–2: K to last st, W&T, p to last st, W&T.
Short Rows 3–4: K to 1 st before wrapped st, W&T, p to 1 st before wrapped st, W&T.
Work Short Rows 3–4 a total of 4 (5, 6) times—6 (8, 10) sts remain unwrapped.
During next section, pick up wraps and work them with st. When a st is double-wrapped, pick up and work both wraps with st.
Return Short Rows 1–2: K to first wrapped st, k wrapped st, W&T, sl 1, p to first wrapped st, p wrapped st, W&T.
Return Short Rows 3–4: Sl 1, k to first double-wrapped st, k double-wrapped st, W&T, sl 1, p to first double-wrapped st, p double-wrapped st, W&T.

Work Return Short Rows 3–4 a total of 3 (4, 5) times; 1 double-wrapped st remains at end of each row.
Next Row: Sl 1, k to double-wrapped st, k double-wrapped st. Do not turn work.
Work wraps on remaining st during next round.
Remove provisional CO and place 16 (20, 24) sts on needles, ready to work—32 (40, 48) sts.
Break yarn. Switch to C.
Knit 2 rounds.
Break yarn. Switch to A.

Foot

Work even until sock measures 4.5 (5.5, 6.5)"/11.5 (14, 16.5) cm from toe. Do not break yarn. Switch to C and knit 2 rounds.

Do not break yarn. Switch to B.

Heel

Heel will be worked back and forth over first 16 (20, 24) sts.

Short Rows 1–2: K15 (19, 23), W&T, p14 (18, 22), W&T.

Short Rows 3–4: K to one st before wrapped st, W&T, p to one st before wrapped st, W&T.

Work Short Rows 3–4 a total of 4 (5, 6) times—6 (8, 10) sts remain unwrapped.

During next section, pick up wraps and work them with st. When a st is double-wrapped, pick up and work both wraps with st.

Return Short Rows 1–2: K to first wrapped st, k wrapped st, W&T, sl 1, p to first wrapped st, p wrapped st, W&T.

Return Short Rows 3–4: Sl 1, k to first double-wrapped st, k double-wrapped st, W&T, sl 1, p to first double-wrapped st, p double-wrapped st, W&T.

Work Return Short Rows 3–4 a total of 3 (4, 5) times, 1 double-wrapped st remains at end of each row.

Next Row: Sl 1, k to double-wrapped st, k double-wrapped st, do not turn work, resume working in the round.

Pick up 1 st at the end of current row, sm, pick up another st, k16 (20, 24), pick up 2 sts before picking up wraps and working wrapped st, k to end of row—36 (44, 52) sts.

Switch to C.

Next Rnd: K2tog, k14 (18, 22), ssk, k2tog, k to last 2 sts, ssk—32 (40, 48) sts.

Knit one round. Switch to A.

Work even in pat until sock measures 4 (5, 6)"/10 (13, 15.25) cm from turn of heel.

Stripe Pattern

Rnds 1–2: Knit in C.

Rnds 3–4: Knit in A.

Rep 4 rounds for pattern.

Work Stripe Pattern three times total. Break yarn for A and C.

Cuff

Switch to B.

Knit 1 round. Switch to smaller needles.

Rib: *K1, p1; rep from * around.

Work in Rib until cuff measures 1"/2.5 cm.

BO all sts with Jeny's Surprisingly Stretchy Bind-Off (see page 28).

Finishing

Weave in all loose ends. Block.

Benson Mittens

There are times when a boy needs access to his fingers, even when it's chilly outside. Climbing, rock piling—those sorts of adventures. Benson is playing in the size Small/Medium.

Size

Standard Size: Small/Medium (Medium/Large)
Finished Circumference: 7 (9.5)"/18 (24) cm

Gauge

18 sts and 24 rows in St st on larger needles = 4"/10 cm square

Yarn

Worsted weight #4 yarn [shown in Skacel HiKoo Simpli-Worsted; 55% merino, 28% acrylic, 17% nylon; 140 yd./128 m per 3.5 oz./100 g skein; Burnt Orange (A), Totally Taupe (B), and Aqua Mint (C)]
- Color A: 100 (135) yd./90 (125) m
- Colors B and C: 25 (35) yd./23 (32) m each

Needles and Other Materials

- US 6 (4 mm) set of 5 double-pointed needles
- US 7 (4.5 mm) set of 5 double-pointed needles
- Stitch marker
- Two 1"/2.5 cm buttons

Wrist and Thumb Opening

With smaller needles and A, CO 32 (40) sts. Place marker and join to work in the round, being careful not to twist stitches.
Rib: *K2, p2; rep from * around.
Work in Rib for 2"/5 cm. Switch to larger needles.
Work in St st until mitten measures 5 (6)"/13 (15) cm from CO edge.

SET-UP FOR THUMB

Left Hand Only
K4 sts, do not break yarn but k5 (6) sts with a length of scrap yarn, sl these 5 (6) sts back to LH needle and resume St st with working yarn to end of round.

Right Hand Only
K to last 9 (10) sts, do not break yarn but k5 (6) sts with a length of scrap yarn, sl these 5 (6) sts back to LH needle and resume St st with working yarn to end of round.

Decreases

Rnd 1: *K6, k2tog; rep from * around—28 (35) sts.
Rnd 2: *K5, k2tog; rep from * around—24 (30) sts.
Rnd 3: *K4, k2tog; rep from * around—20 (25) sts.
Rnd 4: *K3, k2tog; rep from * around—16 (20) sts.
Rnd 5: *K2, k2tog; rep from * around—12 (15) sts.
Rnd 6: *K1, k2tog; rep from * around—8 (10) sts.
Rnd 7: *K2tog; rep from * around—4 (5) sts.
Break yarn, switch to B.
K2tog 1 (2) times—3 sts. Work in I-cord (see page 28) for
10 rounds. BO, leaving a long tail for sewing. Sew end of
I-cord to beginning of I-cord at top of Mitt Cap.

Thumb

Place 5 (6) sts on bottom on single DPN, and 4 (5) sts on top
on second DPN. Carefully pull out scrap yarn for thumb.
Knit sts from bottom DPN. Use a free DPN to pick up and
knit 2 sts in the gap between bottom and top needles,
then knit sts from top DPN. Use another DPN to pick up
and knit 2 sts on other gap. Place marker for end of
round—13 (15) sts.
Rnd 1: K to last 2 sts, k2tog—12 (14) sts.
Rib: *K1, p1; rep from * around.
Work in Rib for 1"/2.5 cm. BO all sts.

Finishing

Weave in all loose ends. Attach button to mitten where Mitt
Cap folds down and meets wrist.

BOTH HANDS

Work in Rib for 1"/2.5 cm. BO all sts.

Mitt Cap

With B, pick up and knit 16 (20) sts along top of mitten
directly underneath ribbing. Cable CO an additional 16
(20) sts—32 (40) sts. Work in Rib for 1 (1.25)"/2.5 (3) cm.
Switch to C. Work in St st for 1 (1.25)"/2.5 (3) cm. Switch
to A. Work in St st for 0 (.25)"/0 (.5) cm.

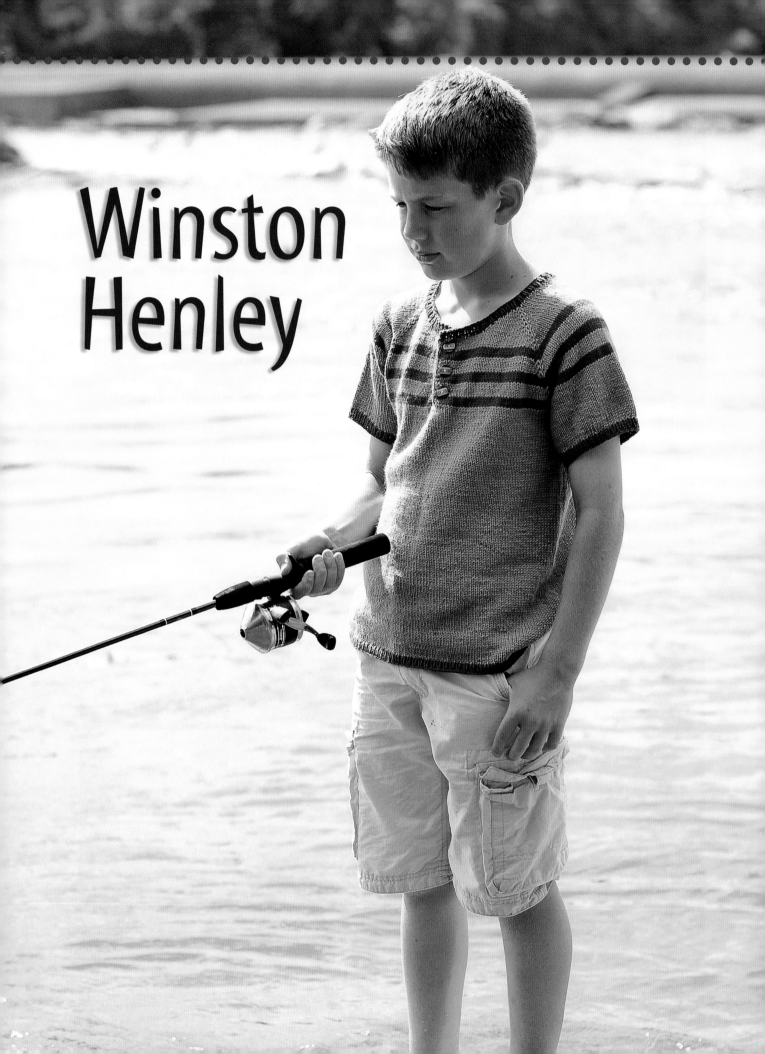

Winston
Henley

ear this tee by itself—make sure to pick a yarn that feels soft against the skin—or put it over long sleeves for a layered look. Pick the perfect buttons and a color combination for your little man's personality and you're set to go with a project that can be customized just for him. Charlie has gone fishin' in the size 12.

Size

Standard Size: 4 (6, 8, 10, 12)
Finished Chest: 24.75 (27, 29, 31.25, 32.75)"/63 (68.5, 74, 79, 83) cm

Gauge

23 sts and 32 rows in St st on larger needles = 4"/10 cm square

Yarn

DK weight #3 yarn [shown in HiKoo by Skacel Simplicity; 55% merino, 28% acrylic, 17% nylon; 117 yd./107 m per 1.5 oz./50 g skein; Periwinkle (A) and Royal Blue (B)]
- Color A: 400 (475, 570, 665, 740) yd./365 (435, 520, 610, 675) m
- Color B: 65 (70, 90, 95, 100) yd./60 (65, 83, 85, 90) m

Needles and Other Materials

- US 4 (3.5 mm) 24"/60 cm circular needle
- US 5 (3.75 mm) 24"/60 cm circular needle
- US 4 (3.5 mm) set of 5 double-pointed needles
- US 5 (3.75 mm) set of 5 double-pointed needles
- US F-5 (3.75 mm) crochet hook
- Stitch markers
- 2 (2, 3, 3, 3) small buttons (ones shown are by Renaissance)

Pattern Notes

- Sweater is worked top-down with raglan-style seamless sleeves back and forth until placket is joined seamlessly, then worked in the round.

Neckline

With larger circular needles, scrap yarn, and crochet hook, provisionally CO 51 (53, 55, 57, 59) sts. Work in St st as follows, purling all WS rows. Begin in A.

Row 1 (WS): P2, pm, p1, pm, p8, pm, p1, pm, p27 (29, 31, 33, 35), pm, p1, pm, p8, pm, p1, pm, p2—27 (29, 31, 33, 35) back sts, 8 sleeve sts, 2 front sts, 4 raglan sts.

Neckline Inc Row (RS): K1, [M1R, k to marker, M1L, sm, k1, sm] 4 times, M1R, k to last st, M1L, k1—10 sts inc.

Work Neckline Inc Row every RS row a total of 6 times—111 (113, 115, 117, 119) sts: 39 (41, 43, 45, 47) back sts, 20 sleeve sts, 14 front sts, 4 raglan sts.

Placket

Note: The following section contains work to be done at the same time. Read through the entire section before beginning. After the placket sts are CO, slip first and last 3 sts of every WS row purlwise, with yarn in front, to create I-cord edge for placket. Knit these sts on RS rows.

Next Row (WS): CO 8 (9, 10, 11, 12) sts, p to end of row.

Next Row (RS): CO 8 (9, 10, 11, 12), [k to marker, M1L, sm, k1, sm, M1R] 4 times, k to last 3 sts, sl 3 sts—135 (139, 143, 147, 151) sts: 41 (43, 45, 47, 49) back sts, 22 sleeves sts, 23 (24, 25, 26, 27) front sts, 4 raglan sts.

Next Row: Sl 3, p to last 3 sts, sl 3.

Stripe Pattern

Rows 1–4: Work in A.
Rows 5–8: Work in B.
Rows 9–10: Work in A.
Rep 10 rows for pat.

Work in Stripe Pattern and *at the same time*, work increases and buttonholes as follows.

Raglan Inc Row (RS): Sl 3, [k to marker, M1L, sm, k1, sm, M1R] 4 times, k to last 3 sts, sl 3 sts—8 sts inc.

Buttonhole Inc Row (RS): Sl 3, k2, work 2-st buttonhole, [k to marker, M1L, sm, k1, sm, M1R] 4 times, k to last 3 sts, sl 3 sts—8 sts inc.

Sequence

Work Raglan Inc Row once, work Buttonhole Inc Row on next RS row, then work Raglan Inc Row every RS row 3 times.

Work Sequence a total of 2 (2, 3, 3, 3) times [10 (10, 15, 15, 15) total Inc rows]—215 (219, 263, 267, 271) sts: 61 (63, 75, 77, 79) back sts, 42 (42, 52, 52, 52) sleeve sts, 33 (34, 40, 41, 42) front sts, 4 raglan sts.

Break yarn for B, continue in A.

Note: Sweater will now be joined to work in the round. You will no longer be slipping sts at the beginning and end of the row.

Sl last 6 sts of the row just worked to spare DPN.

The next row will create the overlap for the placket and join the sweater to be worked in the round. You will be layering 2 sets of stitches on top of one another as indicated and then knitting these stitches together. Make sure that RS is facing on both layers as you work them together.

Joining Row (RS row): Bring DPN holding last 6 sts around and hold behind first 6 sts of the beginning of the row, ready to work RS. [K2tog 1 st from front needle with 1 st from back needle] 6 times, work in pat to end of rnd—209 (213, 257, 261, 265) sts: 61 (63, 75, 77, 79) back sts, 60 (62, 74, 76, 78) front sts, 42 (42, 52, 52, 52) sleeve sts, 4 raglan sts.

Raglan Inc Rnd: [K to marker, M1L, sm, k1, sm, M1R] 4 times, k to end of rnd—8 sts inc.

Work Raglan Inc Rnd every other rnd a total of 2 (3, 0, 1, 3) times—225 (237, 257, 269, 289) sts: 65 (69, 75, 79, 85) back sts, 64 (68, 74, 78, 84) front sts, 46 (48, 52, 54, 58) sleeve sts, 4 raglan sts.

Work even until piece measures 5 (5.5, 6, 6.5, 7)"/13 (14, 15, 16.5, 18) cm from back neck CO edge.

Separate Body and Sleeves

Remove raglan markers during the next round.

Next Row (RS): *Work to marker, k1, sl next 46 (48, 52, 54, 58) sts to hold for sleeve, cable CO 4 (6, 6, 8, 8) underarm sts, rep from *, pm for end of rnd—141 (153, 165, 177, 189) sts.

Work in the round until piece measures 13.75 (15, 17, 18.5, 19.5)"/35 (38, 43, 47, 49.5) cm from back neck CO edge.

Next Rnd: K to last 2 sts, k2tog—140 (152, 164, 176, 188) sts.
Switch to B and smaller needles.
Rib: *K1, p1; rep from * around.
Work in rib for 4 rounds. BO all sts.

Sleeve (Make 2)

Note: Two additional sts are picked up than were CO at under-arm to minimize holes. Make second sleeve same as first.
Place sts for sleeve on DPNs. With spare larger DPN and RS facing, starting at center underarm, pick up and knit 3 (4, 4, 5, 5) sts, knit around 46 (48, 52, 54, 58) sleeve sts, pick up and knit 3 (4, 4, 5, 5) sts, place marker and join to work in the round—52 (56, 60, 64, 68) sts.
Work in the round until sleeve measures 2.5 (2.5, 3, 3, 3)"/6 (6, 7.5, 7.5, 7.5) cm from underarm. Switch to B and smaller DPNs. Work 4 rounds in Rib as for hem. BO all sts.

Collar

Remove provisional CO and place sts on spare needles.
Hold sweater at Right Front with RS facing. With B and smaller needles, pick up and knit 6 (7, 8, 9, 10) sts across right front CO neckline edge, 12 sts along diagonal neckline shaping, knit across provisionally CO sts, pick up and knit 12 sts across left front diagonal neckline shaping and 6 (7, 8, 9, 10) sts along CO neckline edge—91 (95, 99, 103, 107) sts.
Next Row (WS): P1, *k1, p1; rep from * to end of row.
Work 4 rows in rib as for hem and cuffs.
BO all sts in rib.

Finishing

Attach buttons across from buttonholes. Weave in all loose ends. Block.

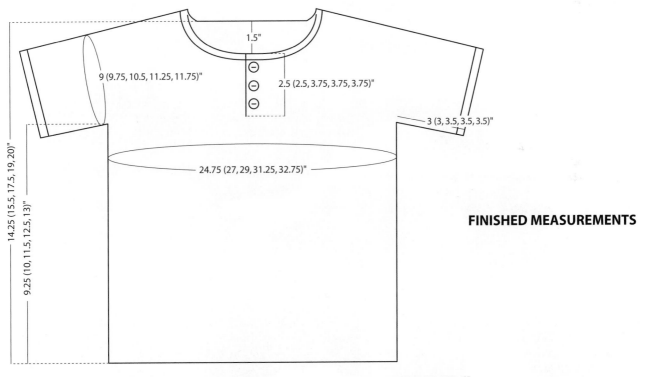

1.5"

9 (9.75, 10.5, 11.25, 11.75)"

2.5 (2.5, 3.75, 3.75, 3.75)"

3 (3, 3.5, 3.5, 3.5)"

24.75 (27, 29, 31.25, 32.75)"

14.25 (15.5, 17.5, 19, 20)"

9.25 (10, 11.5, 12.5, 13)"

FINISHED MEASUREMENTS

Front

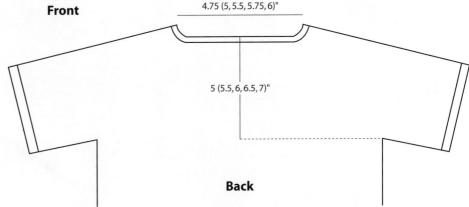

4.75 (5, 5.5, 5.75, 6)"

5 (5.5, 6, 6.5, 7)"

Back

Cooper Hoodie

Before you throw that ratty sweatshirt away, why not knit him a new one that's even better? For the perfect fit, measure his existing top and choose the size here that comes closest. Extra ease is added into this design for a roomier fit. Cooper is riding around outside in the size 8.

Size

Standard Size: 4 (6, 8, 10, 12)
Finished Chest: 25.75 (27.5, 30.25, 32, 34.75)"/65 (70, 77, 81, 88) cm

Gauge

18 sts and 25 rows in St st on larger needles = 4"/10 cm square

Yarn

Worsted weight #4 yarn [shown in Big Bad Wool Weepaca; 50% merino, 50% baby alpaca; 95 yd./86 m per 1.8 oz./50 g skein; Canoe (A) and Fried Egg (B)]
- Color A: 550 (600, 685, 775, 870) yd./500 (550, 625, 710, 795) m
- Color B: 35 (40, 45, 50, 55) yd./32 (37, 41, 46, 50) m

Needles and Other Materials

- US 6 (4 mm) 24"/60 cm circular needle
- US 7 (4.5 mm) 24"/60 cm circular needle
- US 6 (4 mm) set of 5 double-pointed needles
- US 7 (4.5 mm) set of 5 double-pointed needles
- US G-6 (4 mm) crochet hook
- Stitch markers

Pattern Notes

- Sweater is worked top-down with seamless raglan-style sleeves.
- Hood is worked bottom-up beginning at provisionally cast-on edge.

Pocket

With circular needles, crochet hook, and scrap yarn, provisionally CO 36 (38, 40, 42, 44) sts. Work in B. Sl first st of every row.
Row 1 (WS): Purl.
Row 2: Knit.
Purl 1 more row.
Dec Row (RS): Sl 1, ssk, k to last 3 sts, k2tog, k1.
Work Dec Row every four rows a total of 5 (6, 7, 8, 9) times— 26 sts. Place sts on spare DPN and set aside.

Body

With circular needles, crochet hook and scrap yarn, provisionally CO 36 (38, 42, 42, 46) sts. Work in A.
Row 1 (WS): P1, pm, p1, pm, p6, pm, p1, pm, p18 (20, 24, 24, 28), pm, p1, pm, p6, pm, p1, pm, p1.
Inc Row (RS): [K to marker, M1R, sm, k1, sm, M1L] 4 times, k to end of row—8 sts inc.
Purl 1 row.
Neckline Inc Row: K1, M1L, [K to marker, M1R, sm, k1, sm, M1L] 4 times, k to last st, M1R, k1—10 sts inc.
Purl 1 row.
Work last 4 rows twice—72 (74, 78, 78, 82) sts: 26 (28, 32, 32, 36) back sts, 7 front sts, 14 sleeve sts, 4 raglan sts.

Next Row (WS): CO 4 (5, 7, 7, 9) sts, p to end of row.

Next Row (RS): CO 4 (5, 7, 7, 9) sts, [k to marker, M1R, sm, k1, sm, M1L] 4 times, k to end of row—88 (92, 100, 100, 108) sts: 28 (30, 34, 34, 38) back sts, 12 (13, 15, 15, 17) front sts, 16 sleeve sts, 4 raglan sts.

Work Inc Row every RS a total of 9 times more. *Do not turn.*—160 (164, 172, 172, 180) sts: 46 (48, 52, 52, 56) back sts, 21 (22, 24, 24, 26) front sts, 34 sleeve sts, 4 raglan sts.

CO 2 sts, place marker for beginning of round, CO 2 sts and join to work in the round, being careful not to twist sts—164 (168, 176, 176, 184) sts: 46 (48, 52, 52, 56) front/back sts, 34 sleeve sts, 4 raglan sts.

Knit 1 round.

Inc Rnd: [K to marker, M1R, sm, k1, sm, M1L] 4 times, k to end of rnd—8 sts inc.

Work Inc Rnd every other rnd a total of 3 (4, 4, 6, 7) times—188 (200, 208, 224, 240) sts: 52 (56, 60, 64, 70) front/back sts, 40 (42, 42, 46, 48) sleeve sts, 4 raglan sts.

Work even in St st until piece measures 5.5 (6, 6.5, 7, 7.5)"/14 (15.25, 16.5, 17.75, 19) cm from back neck CO edge.

Separate Sleeves from Body

Next Rnd: [K to marker, remove marker, k1, remove marker, sl next 40 (42, 42, 46, 48) sleeve sts to hold, CO 4 (4, 6, 6, 6) sts, remove marker, k1, remove marker] twice, k to end of rnd—116 (124, 136, 144, 156) sts.

Work even in St st until piece measures 9.5 (10.25, 11.5, 12.5, 12.75)"/24 (26, 29, 31.75, 32) cm from back neck CO edge.

Join Pocket to Body

Next Rnd: K to last 13 sts. Hold DPN with top of pocket sts against working needle, RS of pocket facing RS of sweater and WS of pocket facing you. K2tog st from DPN and st from working needle until all sts are joined.

Work even in St st for 20 (24, 28, 32, 36) rounds, or until length matches pocket from top of join. Remove provisional CO from bottom of pocket and place sts on spare DPN, ready to work RS.

Next Rnd: K to last 18 (19, 20, 21, 22) sts. Hold DPN with bottom of pocket sts against working needles, WS of pocket facing RS of sweater and RS of pocket facing you. K2tog st from DPN and st from working needle until all sts are joined.

Knit 2 rounds. Switch to smaller needles.

Rib: *K1, p1; rep from * around.

Work in Rib for 5 rounds. Switch to B.

Knit 1 round.

Work in Rib for 1 round.

BO all sts in Rib.

Sleeve (Make 2)

Note: The total number of sts picked up for the underarm are 2 more than were cast on for the body to minimize holes. Make second sleeve same as first.

Place sts for sleeve on DPNs. With spare DPN and RS facing, starting at center underarm, pick up and knit 3 (3, 4, 4, 4) sts, knit around 40 (42, 42, 46, 48) sleeve sts, pick up and knit 3 (3, 4, 4, 4) sts, place marker and join to work in the round—46 (48, 50, 54, 56) sts.

Knit in the round for 6.75 (5, 3.5, 9, 8)"/17 (13, 9, 23, 20) cm.

Dec Rnd: K1, ssk, k to last 3 sts, k2tog, k1—2 sts dec.

Work Dec Rnd every 2"/5 cm a total of 3 (4, 5, 3, 4) times— 40 (40, 40, 48, 48) sts.

Work even until sleeve measures 11 (11.25, 11.75, 13.25, 14.25)"/28 (28.5, 30, 33.5, 36) cm.

Dec Rnd: *K2, k2tog; rep from * around—30 (30, 30, 36, 36) sts.

Switch to smaller needles.

Rib: *K1, p1; rep from * around.

Work in Rib for 5 rounds. Switch to B.

Knit 1 round.

Work in Rib for 1 round.

BO all sts in Rib.

Hood

Remove provisional CO and place sts on spare needle, ready to work. Starting at right front CO edge (not center front), pick up and knit 4 (5, 7, 7, 9) sts on horizontal CO edge, 6 sts on diagonal edge, knit around 36 (38, 42, 42, 46) neckline sts, pick up and knit 6 sts on left front diagonal edge and 4 (5, 7, 7, 9) sts on horizontal CO edge—56 (60, 68, 68, 76) sts.

Purl 1 WS row.

Inc Row (RS): K1, M1L, k to last st, M1R, k1—2 sts inc.

Work Inc Row every RS row a total of 12 (11, 8, 9, 6) times— 80 (82, 84, 86, 88) sts.

Work even in St st until hood measures 12 (12, 12.5, 12.5, 13)"/30.5 (30.5, 31.75, 31.75, 33) cm. Flip hood inside out and use a three-needle bind-off (see page 30) to seam top closed. Break yarn, weave through rem st and secure.

Finishing

HOOD RIBBING

Starting at center front CO edge, with A and smaller needles, pick up and knit 20 sts along right front vertical placket edge, 108 (108, 112, 112, 116) sts around edges of hood, and 20 sts along left front vertical placket edge— 148 (148, 152, 152, 156) sts.

Rib (WS): *P1, k1; rep from * to end of row.

Rib (RS): *K1, p1; rep from * to end of row.
Work 4 rows total in Rib. Switch to B.
Next Row (WS): Purl.
Work 1 RS row in Rib. BO all sts in Rib.

SEAM

Seam right front ribbed edge to CO center front sts. Layer left front collar on top of right front collar and sew to attach. Weave in all loose ends. Block.

FINISHED MEASUREMENTS

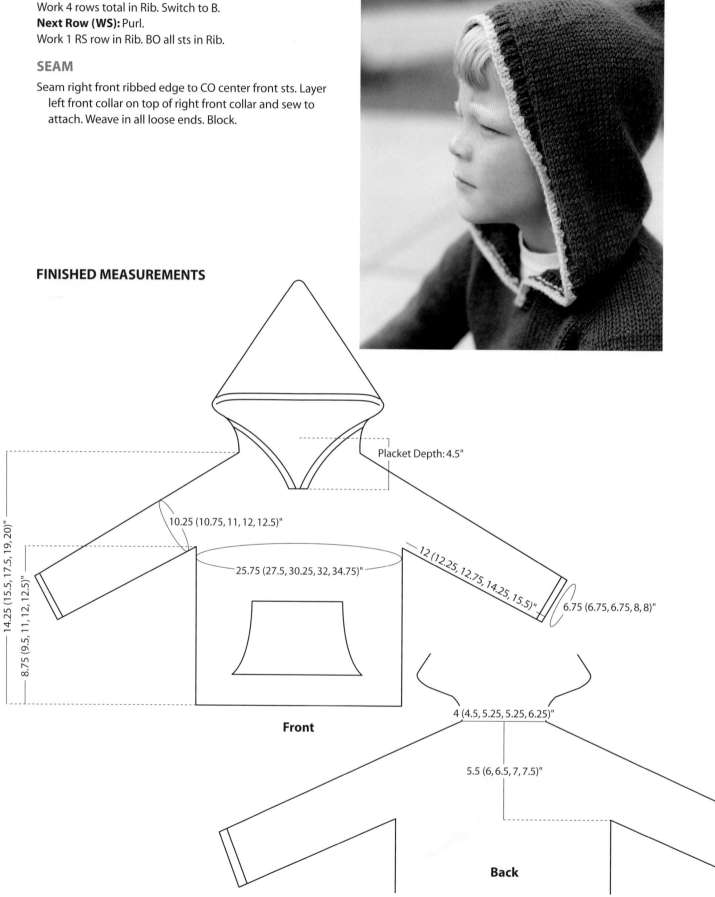

Placket Depth: 4.5"

10.25 (10.75, 11, 12, 12.5)"

25.75 (27.5, 30.25, 32, 34.75)"

14.25 (15.5, 17.5, 19, 20)"

8.75 (9.5, 11, 12, 12.5)"

12 (12.25, 12.75, 14.25, 15.5)"

6.75 (6.75, 6.75, 8, 8)"

Front

4 (4.5, 5.25, 5.25, 6.25)"

5.5 (6, 6.5, 7, 7.5)"

Back

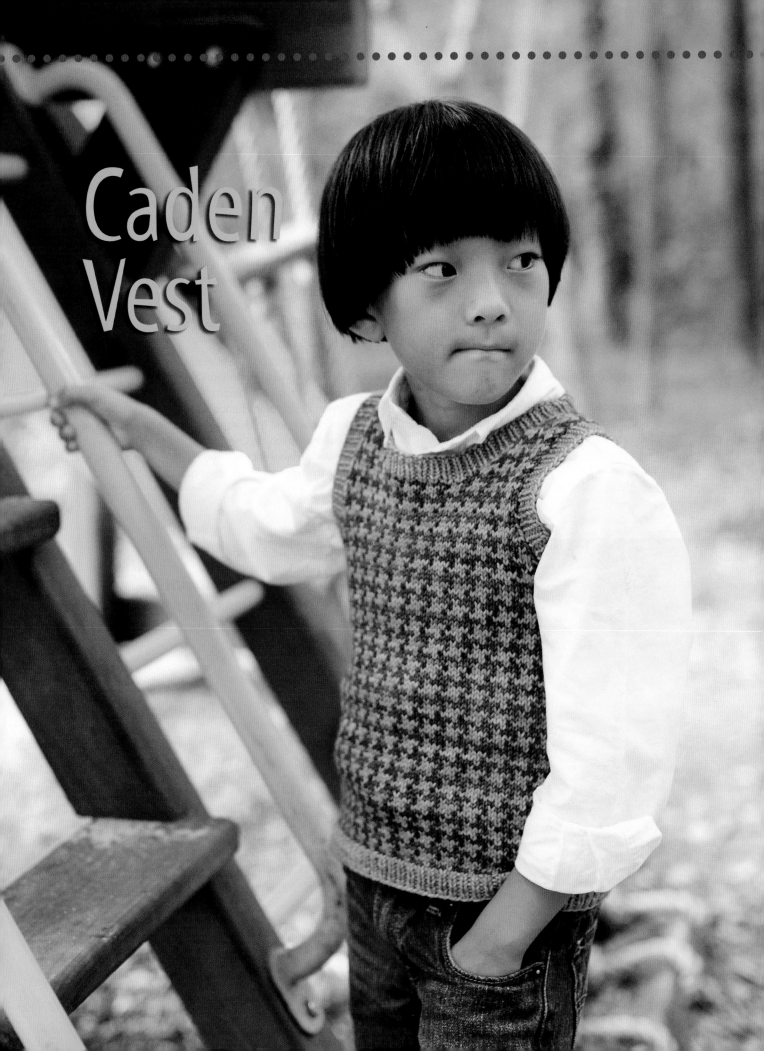

Caden Vest

n my experience, a classic colorwork motif combined with funky colors makes for a happy boy. Layer it with short sleeves, too. You'll memorize this easy four-stitch pattern quickly. Caden is dressed to impress in the size 4.

Size

Standard Size: 4 (6, 8, 10, 12)
Finished Chest: 25.25 (26.75, 28.25, 30.5, 32.75)"/56.5 (68, 73, 77.5, 83) cm

Gauge

21 sts and 28 rows in St st on larger needles = 4"/10 cm square

Yarn

DK to light worsted weight #3 yarn [shown in Madelinetosh Tosh DK; 100% merino; 225 yd./206 m per 3.5 oz./100 g skein; Grasshopper (A) and Denim (B)]
- Color A: 250 (285, 340, 400, 440) yd./230 (260, 310, 365, 400) m
- Color B: 195 (225, 275, 325, 370) yd./180 (205, 250, 300, 340) m

Needles and Other Materials

- US 6 (4 mm) 24"/60 cm circular needle
- US 7 (4.5 mm) 24"/60 cm circular needle
- Stitch marker

Pattern Notes

- Vest is worked bottom-up.
- You will need to be able to read your work and make adjustments to the colorwork stitch pattern once shaping for the armholes begins.
- Sometimes tension changes when knitting in the round versus back and forth, especially when there is stranded colorwork involved. Consider swatching both ways to determine whether you should adjust your needle size once the front and back are separated.

Stitch Guide

Rib

*K1, p1; rep from * around.

Houndstooth

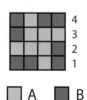

☐ A ◼ B

Houndstooth (worked in the round over a multiple of 4 sts)

Rnd 1: *With B, k1, with A, k1, with B, k2; rep from * around.
Rnd 2: *With B, k1, with A, k3; rep from * around.
Rnd 3: *With A, k3, with B, k1; rep from * around.
Rnd 4: *With B, k2, with A, k1, with B, k1; rep from * around.
Rep 4 rounds for pattern.

Houndstooth (worked back and forth over a multiple of 4 sts)

Row 1 (RS): *With B, k1, with A, k1, with B, k2; rep from * to end of row.
Row 2: *With A, p3, with B, p1; rep from * to end of row.
Row 3: *With A, k3, with B, k1; rep from * to end of row.
Row 4: *With B, p1, with A, p1, with B, p2; rep from * to end of row.
Rep 4 rows for pattern.

Body

Using smaller circular needles and A, CO 132 (140, 148, 160, 172) sts using the long-tail cast-on method. Place marker and join in the round, being careful not to twist stitches. Work in Rib for 1"/2.5 cm. Switch to larger needles.

Work Houndstooth in the round until sweater measures 8.75 (9.75, 11.25, 12.25, 12.75)"/22 (25, 28.5, 31, 32) cm from CO edge. Front and back will be worked separately back and forth. Continue working in Houndstooth back and forth throughout shaping of the Back and Front(s).

Back

Row 1 (RS): BO 5 (6, 6, 6, 7) sts, work 60 (63, 67, 73, 78) sts in pat—61 (64, 68, 74, 79) sts.

Place remaining 66 (70, 74, 80, 86) sts on hold for front.

Row 2 (WS): BO 5 (6, 6, 6, 7) sts, work in pat to end.

Dec Row (RS): K1, ssk, work in pat to last 3 sts, k2tog, k1—2 sts dec.

Work Dec Row every RS row a total of 6 (6, 7, 8, 8) times—44 (46, 48, 52, 56) sts.

Continue working back and forth in Houndstooth until armhole measures 5.5 (5.75, 6.25, 6.75, 7.25)"/14 (14.5, 16, 17, 18) cm, ending after Row 2 of Houndstooth.

Place sts on hold.

Front

Place front sts on needle, ready to work RS.

Row 1 (RS): BO 5 (6, 6, 6, 7) sts, work in pat to end.

Row 2 (WS): BO 5 (6, 6, 6, 7) sts, work in pat to end.

Dec Row (RS): K1, ssk, work in pat to last 3 sts, k2tog, k1—2 sts dec.

Work Dec Row every RS row a total of 6 (6, 7, 8, 8) times—44 (46, 48, 52, 56) sts.

Continue working back and forth in Houndstooth until armhole measures 3 (3, 3.25, 3.5, 3.75)"/7.5 (7.5, 8.25, 8.25, 9.5) cm, ending after a WS row.

Neck Shaping

Row 1: Work 14 (15, 15, 17, 18) sts before center front, sl next 16 (16, 18, 18, 20) sts to scrap yarn or holder, join second ball of yarn, work in pat to end.

Row 2 and all WS rows: Work in pat.

Row 3: Work to 3 sts before center, k2tog, k1, pick up second ball, k1, ssk, knit to end.

Repeat the last 2 rows 6 more times—7 (8, 8, 10, 11) sts for each shoulder.

Work until armhole measures same as for back, ending after Row 2 of Houndstooth.

Place back sts on other side of needle so that the RS of the vest are facing each other.

Use three-needle bind-off (see page 30) to seam 7 (8, 8, 10, 11) sts for shoulders closed, place 30 (30, 32, 32, 34) sts on hold for back neck, use three-needle bind-off to seam remaining sts.

Finishing

NECKLINE

Place front collar sts on spare DPN. Place 30 (30, 32, 32, 34) back neck sts on needle ready to work RS. Using smaller needles and A, knit across these sts. Pick up and knit 15 (16, 17, 18, 19) sts on the left side of the collar, then knit across 16 (16, 18, 18, 20) front collar sts. Pick up and knit another 15 (16, 17, 18, 19) sts on the right side of the collar—76 (78, 84, 86, 92) sts. Place marker and join to work in the round. Work in Rib for 5 rounds. BO loosely in rib.

ARMBANDS

With RS facing, smaller needles, and A, pick up and knit 68 (72, 78, 84, 92) sts around each armhole. Work in Rib for 5 rounds. BO loosely in rib.

Weave in loose ends. Block.

FINISHED MEASUREMENTS

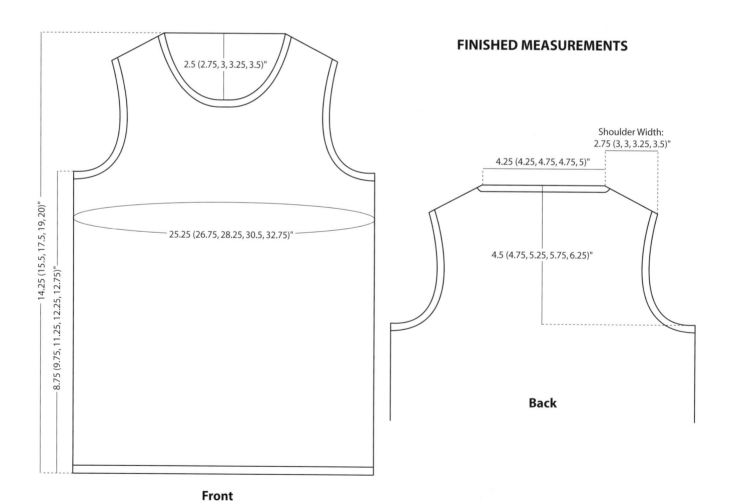

2.5 (2.75, 3, 3.25, 3.5)"

25.25 (26.75, 28.25, 30.5, 32.75)"

14.25 (15.5, 17.5, 19, 20)"

8.75 (9.75, 11.25, 12.25, 12.75)"

Front

Shoulder Width: 2.75 (3, 3, 3.25, 3.5)"

4.25 (4.25, 4.75, 4.75, 5)"

4.5 (4.75, 5.25, 5.75, 6.25)"

Back

Big Bad Vest

A pop of bright colors accents this otherwise muted chevron vest. If stranded colorwork makes you nervous, simplify this design by working stripes instead of chevrons. Jesse is reading in the size 8.

Size

Standard Size: 4 (6, 8, 10, 12)
Finished Chest: 25.25 (26.75, 28.25, 30.5, 32.75)"/64 (68, 71.75, 77.5, 83) cm

Gauge

21 sts and 26 rows in St st on larger needles = 4"/10 cm square

Yarn

DK to light worsted weight #3 yarn [shown in Big Bad Wool Weepaca; 50% merino, 50% baby alpaca; 95 yd./86 m per 1.8 oz./50 g skein; Water (A), Ashes (B), and Fried Egg (C)]

- Colors A and B: 195 (225, 275, 325, 370) yd./180 (205, 250, 300, 340) m
- Color C: 65 (70, 75, 80, 85) yd./60 (65, 68, 73, 77) m

Needles and Other Materials

- US 5 (3.75 mm) 24"/60 cm circular needle
- US 6 (4 mm) 24"/60 cm circular needle
- Stitch marker

Pattern Notes

- Vest is worked bottom-up.
- You will need to be able to read your work and make adjustments to the colorwork stitch pattern once shaping for the armholes begins.
- Sometimes tension changes when knitting in the round versus back and forth, especially when there is stranded colorwork involved. Consider swatching both ways to determine whether you should adjust your needle size once the front and back are separated.

Stitch Guide

Rib

*K1, p1; rep from * around.

Chevron (worked in the round over a multiple of 4 sts)

Rnds 1–2: With A, knit.
Rnd 3: *With A, k2, with B, k1, with A, k1; rep from * around.
Rnd 4: *With A, k1, with B, k3; rep from * around.
Rnds 5–6: With B, knit.
Rnd 7: *With B, k2, with A, k1, with B, k1; rep from * around.
Rnd 8: *With B, k1, with A, k3; rep from * around.
Rep 8 rounds for pattern.

Chevron (worked back and forth over a multiple of 4 sts)

Rows 1 (RS)–2: Work in A.
Row 3: *With A, k2, with B, k1, with A, k1; rep from * to end of row.
Row 4: *With B, p3, with A, p1; rep from * to end of row.
Rows 5–6: Work in B.
Row 7: *With B, k2, with A, k1, with B, k1; rep from * around.
Row 8: *With A, p3, with B, p1; rep from * around.
Rep 8 rows for pattern.

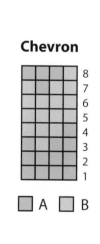

Chevron

Body

Using smaller circular needles and C, CO 132 (140, 148, 160, 172) sts using the long-tail cast-on method. Place marker and join in the round, being careful not to twist stitches. Work in Rib for 1"/2.5 cm. Switch to larger needles.

Work Chevron in the round until sweater measures 8.75 (9.75, 11.25, 12.25, 12.75)"/22 (25, 28.5, 31, 32) cm from CO edge. Front and back will be worked separately back and forth. Continue working in Chevron back and forth throughout shaping of the Back and Front(s).

Back

Row 1 (RS): BO 5 (6, 6, 6, 7) sts, work 60 (63, 67, 73, 78) sts in pat—61 (64, 68, 74, 79) sts.

Place remaining 66 (70, 74, 80, 86) sts on hold for front.

Row 2 (WS): BO 5 (6, 6, 6, 7) sts, work in pat to end.

Dec Row (RS): K1, ssk, work in pat to last 3 sts, k2tog, k1—2 sts dec.

Work Dec Row every RS row a total of 6 (6, 7, 8, 8) times—44 (46, 48, 52, 56) sts.

Continue working back and forth in Chevron Pattern until armhole measures 5.5 (5.75, 6.25, 6.75, 7.25)"/14 (14.5, 16, 17, 18) cm, ending after Row 1 or Row 5 of Chevron Pattern.

Place sts on hold.

Front

Place front sts on needle, ready to work RS.

Row 1 (RS): BO 5 (6, 6, 6, 7) sts, work in pat to end.

Row 2 (WS): BO 5 (6, 6, 6, 7) sts, work in pat to end.

Dec Row (RS): K1, ssk, work in pat to last 3 sts, k2tog, k1—2 sts dec.

Work Dec Row every RS row a total of 6 (6, 7, 8, 8) times—44 (46, 48, 52, 56) sts.

Continue working back and forth in Chevron until armhole measures 3 (3, 3.25, 3.5, 3.75)"/7.5 (7.5, 8.25, 9, 9.5) cm, ending after a RS row.

Neck Shaping

Row 1 (WS): Work 22 (23, 24, 26, 28) sts before center front, join second ball of yarn, work in pat to end.

Neckline Shaping Row (RS): Work to 3 sts before center, k2tog, k1, pick up second ball, k1, ssk, knit to end.

Work Neckline Shaping Row on every RS row a total of 15 (15, 16, 16, 17) times—7 (8, 8, 10, 11) sts for each shoulder.

Work until armhole measures same as for back, ending on same row of Chevron as for back.

Place back sts on other side of needle so that the RS of the vest are facing each other.

Use three-needle bind-off (see page 30) to seam 7 (8, 8, 10, 11) sts for shoulders closed, place 30 (30, 32, 32, 34) sts on hold for back neck, use three-needle bind-off to seam remaining sts.

Finishing

NECKLINE

Place front collar sts on spare DPN. Place 30 (30, 32, 32, 34) back neck sts on needle ready to work RS. Using smaller needles and C, knit across these sts. Pick up and knit 15 (16, 17, 18, 19) sts on the left side of the collar, pm, then knit across 16 (16, 18, 18, 20) front collar sts. Pick up and knit another 15 (16, 17, 18, 19) sts on the right side of the collar—76 (78, 84, 86, 92) sts. Place marker and join to work in the round.

Dec Rib: Work in Rib to 2 sts before marker, ssk, sm, k2tog, work in Rib to end of round—2 sts dec.

Work Dec Rib every round a total of 4 times—68(70, 76, 78, 84) sts.

BO loosely in rib.

ARMBANDS

With RS facing, smaller needles, and A, pick up and knit 68 (72, 78, 84, 92) sts around each armhole. Work in Rib for 4 rounds. BO loosely in rib.

Weave in loose ends. Block.

FINISHED MEASUREMENTS

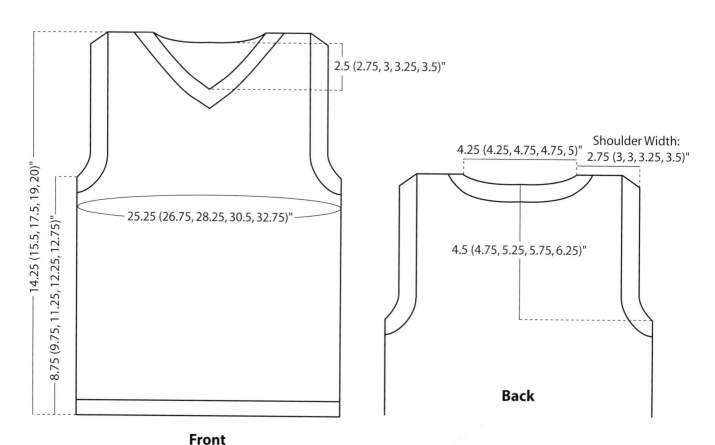

2.5 (2.75, 3, 3.25, 3.5)"

14.25 (15.5, 17.5, 19, 20)"

8.75 (9.75, 11.25, 12.25, 12.75)"

25.25 (26.75, 28.25, 30.5, 32.75)"

4.25 (4.25, 4.75, 4.75, 5)"

Shoulder Width: 2.75 (3, 3, 3.25, 3.5)"

4.5 (4.75, 5.25, 5.75, 6.25)"

Back

Front

Stranded Newsie

brim for a little shade and a modern print for a little style make this cap too cool. This project is on the adventurous side with short-row shaping and some stranded colorwork involved but there is truly no project better suited to practice new techniques than a hat. Charlie is wearing size Child. Size up or add extra length in the body for a more slouchy fit.

Size

Standard Size: Child (Adult Small)
Finished Circumference: 18.5 (21.5)"/27 (54.5) cm

Gauge

26 sts and 36 rows in St st = 4"/10 cm square

Yarn

Sport weight #2 yarn [shown in Skacel Zitron Unisono; 100% merino; 328 yd./300 m per 3.5 oz./100 g skein; Canary (A) and Olive (B)]
- Color A: 135 (165) yd./125 (150) m
- Color B: 120 (150) yd./110 (140) m

Needles and Other Materials

- US 4 (3.5 mm) 16"/40 cm circular needle
- US 4 (3.5 mm) set of 5 double-pointed needles
- Stitch markers
- Plastic template or other suitable washable brim material

Pattern Notes

- This hat is worked bottom-up and the brim is shaped with short rows.

Brim

With B and circular needles, CO 120 (140) sts. Place marker and join to work in the round, being careful not to twist sts.
Knit 3 rounds.
Next Rnd: K40 (50), pm, k40, pm, k to end of rnd.

Short-Row Shaping

Short Rows 1–2: K to second marker, W&T, p to marker, W&T.

Short Rows 3–4: K to 1 st before wrapped st, W&T, p to 1 st before wrapped st, W&T.

Work Short Rows 3–4 once more.

Knit to end of round, picking up wraps and knitting them together with the wrapped st.

Turning Rnd: P 1 round, picking up rem wraps and purling them together with the wrapped st.

Short Rows 1–2: K to 2 sts before second marker, W&T, p to 2 sts before marker, W&T.

Short Rows 3 –4: Sl 1, k to wrapped st, k wrapped st together with wrap, W&T, sl 1, p to wrapped st, p wrapped st together with wrap, W&T.

Work Short Rows 3–4 once more.

Knit to end of round, picking up wrap and knitting wrapped st together with wrap. During next round, pick up rem wrap and knit wrapped st together with wrap.

Knit 3 rounds.

BRIM CASING

Note: A gap is created in the casing in order to slip brim material inside hat once finished knitting.

Joining Rnd: Fold the brim section in half toward the inside of the hat so that Turning Rnd becomes bottom of hat. Join brim sts to CO edge as follows: *pick up the first st from the CO edge, purl next st tog with corresponding st on CO edge**; rep from * to ** to first marker, remove marker, repeat from * to ** to 6 sts before next marker, k6 sts and *do not join* them, remove marker, rep from * to ** to end of rnd.

Hat Body

Switch to A. Do not break yarn for B.

Inc Rnd: *K6 (7), M1L; rep from * around—140 (160) sts.

Diamonds (worked over a multiple of 4 sts)

Rnd 1: *With A, k3, with B, k1; rep from * around.
Rnd 2: *With B, k1, with A, k1; rep from * around.
Rnd 3: *With A, k1, with B, k1, with A, k2; rep from * around.
Rnd 4: *With B, k1, with A, k1; rep from * around.

Rep 4 rounds for pattern.

Work in Diamonds until hat measures 6 (6.75)"/15 (17) cm from bottom of hat (Turning Rnd).

Diamonds

□ A ■ B

Crown Shaping

Note: Continue working Diamonds in each decrease section to last 2 sts. However, always work k2tog in B regardless of whether it is the patterned color.
Set-Up Rnd: *Work 20 sts in pat, pm; rep from * around.
Dec Rnd: *Work in pat to 2 sts before marker, with B, k2tog; rep from * around—7 (8) sts dec.
Work Dec Rnd every rnd a total of 19 times—7 (8) sts. Break yarn, weave through rem sts and secure.

Finishing

Trace brim template on a piece of paper first, cut it out and see how it fits around your little man's forehead. Adjust the shape of the inside curve if necessary. Then, trace your new paper template on your brim material and cut it out. If you are not able to test the brim on its recipient, you can always adjust the brim material later on if necessary. Slip brim material inside casing. Sew gap in casing closed. Weave in all loose ends. Block.

Brim Template

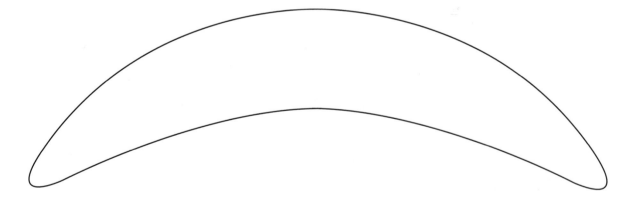

T. Rex Graphic Pullover

A skiing T. rex accents this otherwise basic sweater. The intarsia is worked "in the round" with a wrap and turn technique that allows you to insert a graphic without having to add a seam. Jesse is pulling his little brothers in the size 8.

Size

Standard Size: 4 (6, 8, 10, 12)
Finished Chest: 25.25 (27, 29.5, 31.25, 32.75)"/64 (68.5, 75, 79, 83) cm

Gauge

19 sts and 28 rows in St st = 4"/10 cm square

Yarn

Worsted weight #4 yarn [shown in Spud and Chloë Sweater (55% wool, 45% organic cotton; 160 yd./146 m per 3.5 oz./100 g skein; Beluga (A), Grass (B), Cider (C), and Penguin (D)]

- Color A: 500 (560, 680, 785, 900) yd./460 (510, 620, 720, 825) m
- Color B: 30 yd./27 m
- Colors C and D: scrap amounts

Needles and Other Materials

- US 7 (4.5 mm) 24"/60 cm circular needle
- US 7 (4.5 mm) set of 5 double-pointed needles
- US G-6 (4 mm) crochet hook
- Stitch markers

Pattern Notes

- Sweater is worked top-down with seamless raglan-style sleeves.
- Use duplicate stitch for color D instead of working it intarsia.
- Before beginning chart work, set up bobbins as follows: two for B, one with 25 yd./23 m and the other with 5 yd./4.5 m, and two for C with equal amounts of scrap yarn, no more than a yard each.

Body

With circular needles, crochet hook, and scrap yarn, provisionally CO 36 (38, 40, 42, 42) sts. Work in A.

Row 1 (WS): P1, pm, p1, pm, p4, pm, p1, pm, p22 (24, 26, 28, 28), pm, p1, pm, p4, pm, p1, pm, p1.

Inc Row: [K to marker, M1R, sm, k1, sm, M1L] 4 times, k to end of row—8 sts inc.

Purl 1 row.

Neckline Inc Row: K1, M1L, [K to marker, M1R, sm, k1, sm, M1L] 4 times, k to last st, M1R, k1—10 sts inc.

Purl 1 row.

Work last 4 rows once more—72 (74, 76, 78, 78) sts: 30 (32, 34, 36, 36) back sts, 7 front sts, 12 sleeve sts, 4 raglan sts.

Next Row (RS): CO 16 (18, 20, 22, 22) sts, [k to marker, M1R, sm, k1, sm, M1L] 4 times, k to end of row, join to work in the round, being careful not to twist sts, k to fourth marker, place marker for end of rnd—96 (100, 104, 108, 108) sts: 32 (34, 36, 38, 38) front/back sts, 14 sleeve sts, 4 raglan sts.

Knit 1 round.

Inc Rnd: [K to marker, M1R, sm, k1, sm, M1L] 4 times, k to end of rnd—8 sts inc.

Work Inc Rnd every other rnd a total of 12 times—192 (196, 200, 204, 204) sts: 56 (58, 60, 62, 62) front/back sts, 38 sleeve sts, 4 raglan sts.

Next Rnd: K to fourth marker, k6 (7, 8, 6, 6) place marker for chart, k44 (44, 44, 50, 50), place marker for end of chart, k to end of rnd.

Note: Continue working in St st, knitting all sts worked on the RS and purling sts worked on the WS.

Increase with intarsia in the round: [K to marker, M1R, sm, k1, sm, M1L] twice, k to marker, work chart to next marker, [K to marker, M1R, sm, k1, sm, M1L] twice, k to end of rnd, W&T, p to fifth marker, work chart to next marker, p to end of rnd, W&T.

Work Increase with Intarsia a total of 0 (1, 2, 3, 5) times—192 (204, 216, 228, 244) sts: 56 (60, 64, 68, 72) back/front sts, 38 (40, 42, 44, 48) sleeve sts, 4 raglan sts.

Intarsia in the round: K to fifth marker, work chart to next marker, k to end of rnd, W&T, p to fifth marker, work chart to next marker, p to end of rnd, W&T.

Work Intarsia in the round and *at the same time*, separate body from sleeves when piece measures 5 (5.5, 6, 6.5, 7)"/13 (14, 15, 16.5, 18) cm from back neck CO edge, ending after a return row.

Sizes 4 (6, 8)

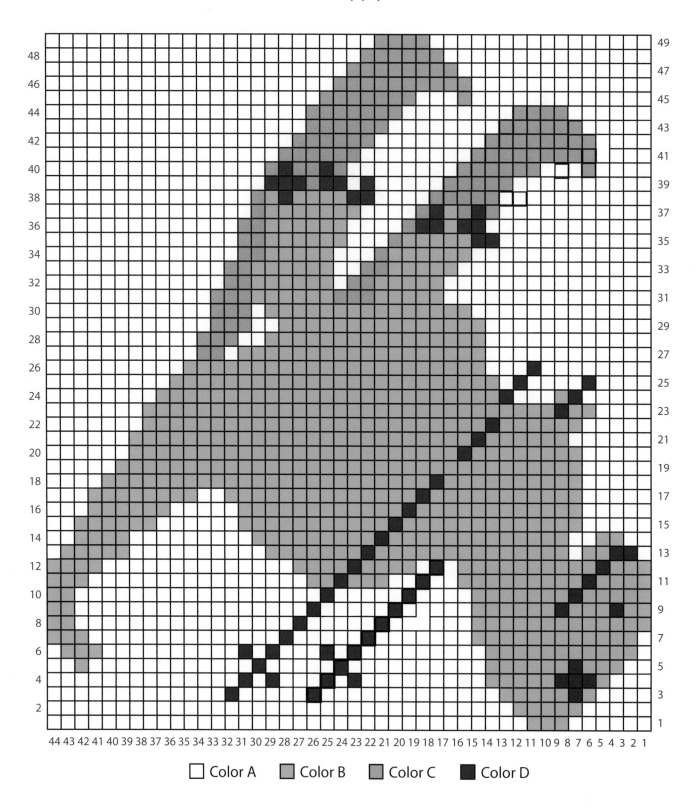

Color A   Color B   Color C   Color D

Sizes (10, 12)

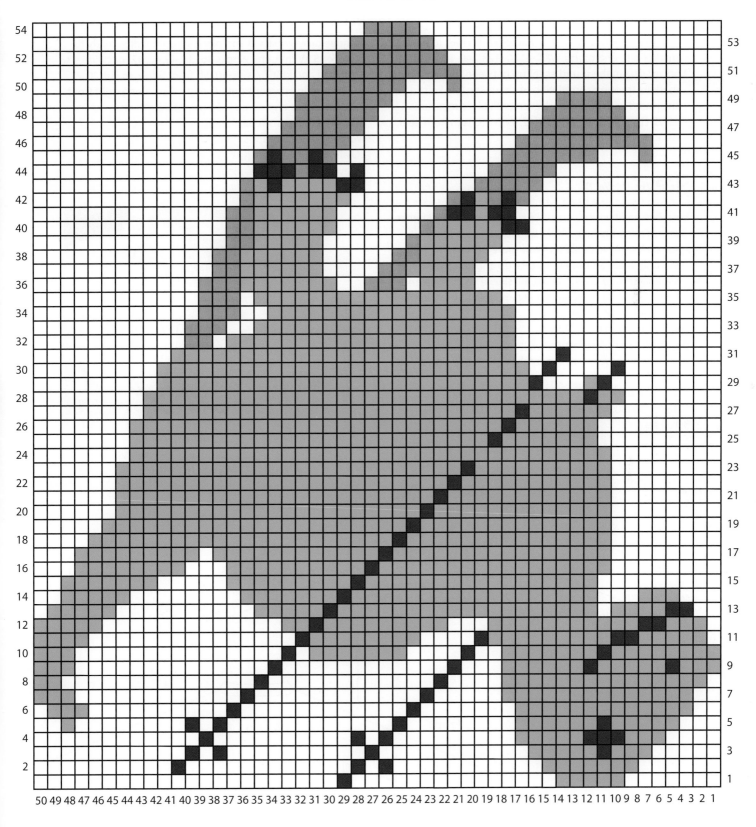

☐ Color A   ▥ Color B   ▨ Color C   ■ Color D

SEPARATE BODY AND SLEEVES

Next Rnd: *K to marker, remove marker, sl next 40 (42, 44, 46, 50) sts to hold, removing markers, CO 4 (4, 6, 6, 6) sts, ** k to marker, work chart to next marker, repeat from * to **, k to end of rnd, W&T, p to marker, work chart to next marker, p to end of rnd, W&T—120 (128, 140, 148, 156) sts.

Work intarsia in the round as set up between the remaining markers through completion of chart. Resume knitting in the round with A and work even until piece measures 15.25 (16.5, 18.5, 20, 21)"/39 (42, 47, 51, 53) cm from back neck CO edge. BO all sts.

Sleeve (Make 2)

Note: Two additional sts are picked up than were CO at under-arm to minimize holes. Make second sleeve same as first.

Place sts for sleeve on DPNs. With spare DPN and RS facing, starting at center underarm, pick up and knit 3 (3, 4, 4, 4) sts, knit around 40 (42, 44, 46, 50) sleeve sts, pick up and knit 3 (3, 4, 4, 4) sts, place marker and join to work in the round—46 (48, 52, 54, 58) sts.

Knit in the round for 1"/2.5 cm.

Dec Rnd: K1, ssk, k to last 3 sts, k2tog, k1—2 sts dec.

Work Dec Rnd every 9 rnds a total of 7 (7, 7, 8, 9) times—32 (34, 36, 38, 40) sts.

Work even until sleeve measures 11.75 (12, 12.75, 14, 15.5)"/30 (30.5, 32, 35.5, 39) cm.

BO all sts.

Finishing

NECKLINE

Remove provisional CO and place sts on needles, ready to work RS. With A, knit across 36 (38, 40, 42, 42) neckline sts, pick up and knit 7 sts along left front edge, 16 (18, 20, 22, 22) sts along center front CO edge, 7 sts along right front edge, pm for end of rnd—66 (70, 74, 78, 78) sts.

Rib: *K1, p1; rep from * around.

Work in Rib for 5 rounds.

BO all sts.

Weave in all loose ends. Block.

FINISHED MEASUREMENTS

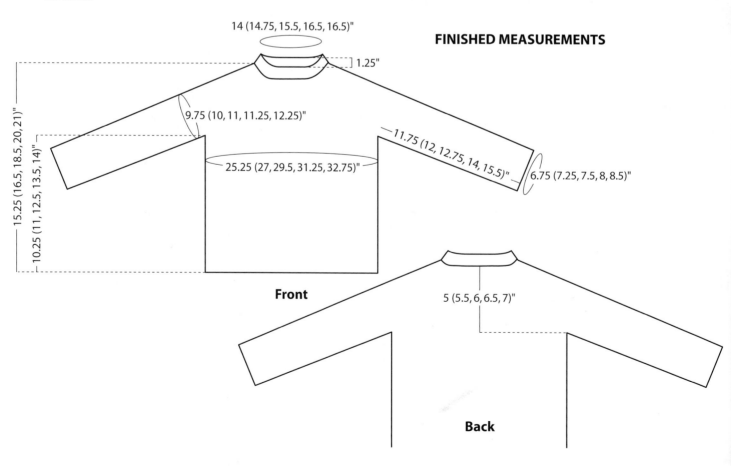

14 (14.75, 15.5, 16.5, 16.5)"

1.25"

9.75 (10, 11, 11.25, 12.25)"

11.75 (12, 12.75, 14, 15.5)"

25.25 (27, 29.5, 31.25, 32.75)"

6.75 (7.25, 7.5, 8, 8.5)"

15.25 (16.5, 18.5, 20, 21)"

10.25 (11, 12.5, 13.5, 14)"

Front

5 (5.5, 6, 6.5, 7)"

Back

Imagination
Sweater

t's cozy at the neck and colorful all the way down. Choose your favorite stitch patterns from the many provided options or, for a more basic sweater, stripe it instead. Charlie is king of the forest in the size 6.

Size

Standard Size: 4 (6, 8, 10, 12)
Finished Chest: 24.75 (27.25, 28.75, 31.25, 32.75)"/63 (69, 73, 79, 83) cm

Gauge

20 sts and 26 rows in St st = 4"/10 cm square

Yarn

Worsted weight #4 yarn [shown in HiKoo by Skacel Kenzie [50% wool, 25% nylon, 10% angora, 10% alpaca; 160 yd./146 m per 1.8 oz./50 g skein; Kumara (A), Manuka (B), Kale (C), Kiwano (D), Oceania (E), and Bayberry (F)]

- Color A: 330 (370, 430, 490, 565) yd./300 (340, 395, 450, 515) m
- Color B: 125 (130, 140, 150, 160) yd./115 (120, 130, 140, 145) m
- Colors C, D, E, and F: 35 (45, 60, 70, 80) yd./32 (41, 55, 65, 73) m

Needles and Other Materials

- US 6 (4 mm) 24"/60 cm circular needle
- US 7 (4.5 mm) 24"/60 cm circular needle
- US 6 (4 mm) set of 5 double-pointed needles
- US 7 (4.5 mm) set of 5 double-pointed needles
- US G-6 (4 mm) crochet hook
- Stitch markers
- Yarn needle
- 1 large button

Pattern Notes

- Sweater is worked top-down with seamless raglan-style sleeves.
- Collar is picked up and worked with short-row shaping.

Body

With circular needles, crochet hook, and scrap yarn, provisionally CO 33 (37, 37, 41, 41) sts. Work in A.

Row 1 (WS): P1, pm, p1, pm, p4, pm, p1, pm, p19 (23, 23, 27, 27), pm, p1, pm, p4, pm, p1, pm, p1.

Inc Row (RS): [K to marker, M1R, sm, k1, sm, M1L] 4 times, k to end of row—8 sts inc.

Purl 1 row.

Neckline Inc Row: K1, M1L, [K to marker, M1R, sm, k1, sm, M1L] 4 times, k to last st, M1R, k1—10 sts inc.

Purl 1 row.

Work last 4 rows a total of 2 (4, 4, 6, 6) times—69 (109, 109, 149, 149) sts: 27 (39, 39, 51, 51) back sts, 7 (13, 13, 19, 19) front sts, 12 (20, 20, 28, 28) sleeve sts, 4 raglan sts.

Work Inc Row every RS row a total of 10 (6, 8, 4, 6) more times. *Do not turn.*—149 (157, 173, 181, 197) sts: 47 (51, 55, 59, 63) back sts, 17 (19, 21, 23, 25) front sts, 32 (32, 36, 36, 40) sleeve sts, 4 raglan sts.

Cable CO 11 sts. Join sts to work in the round. Knit to fourth marker, place marker for end of round—160 (168, 184,

192, 208) sts: 47 (51, 55, 59, 63) back sts, 45 (49, 53, 57, 61) front sts, 32 (32, 36, 36, 40) sleeve sts, 4 raglan sts.

Inc Rnd: [K to marker, M1R, sm, k1, sm, M1L] 4 times, k to end of rnd—8 sts inc.

Work Inc Rnd every other rnd a total of 5 (5, 5, 6, 6) times—200 (208, 224, 240, 256) sts: 57 (61, 65, 71, 75) back sts, 55 (59, 63, 69, 73) front sts, 42 (42, 46, 48, 52) sleeve sts, 4 raglan sts.

Work even in St st until piece measures 5 (5.5, 6, 6.5, 7)"/13 (14, 15, 16.5, 18) cm from back neck CO edge.

SEPARATE SLEEVES FROM BODY

Next Rnd: [K to marker, remove marker, k1, remove marker, sl next 42 (42, 46, 48, 52) sleeve sts to hold, CO 4 (6, 6, 6, 6) sts, remove marker, k1, remove marker] twice, k to end of rnd—124 (136, 144, 156, 164) sts.

Knit 4 rounds.

Colorwork Sequence

Rnd 1: Knit in B.

Rnds 2–6: Work from Chart.

Work in Colorwork Sequence using the charts of your choice for a total of 7 (8, 10, 11, 12) charts. Piece should measure approximately 12 (13.5, 15.75, 17.25, 18.5)"/30.5 (34, 40, 44, 47) cm from back neck CO edge. Work additional chart(s) if necessary to match length. Charts 1–8

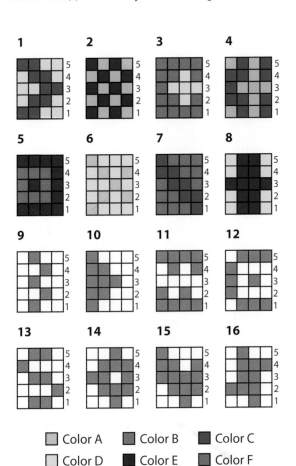

Color A   Color B   Color C
Color D   Color E   Color F

are numbered according to how they are shown in sample, so work chronologically should you choose to match it. Charts 9–16 are not shown in sample sweater.

Switch to B and smaller needles. Knit 1 round.

Rib: *K1, p1; rep from * around.

Work in Rib for 2"/5 cm.

BO all sts.

Sleeve (Make 2)

Note: Two additional sts are picked up than were CO at underarm to minimize holes. Make second sleeve same as first.

Place sts for sleeve on DPNs. With spare larger DPN, RS facing and A, starting at center underarm, pick up and knit 3 (4, 4, 4, 4) sts, knit around 42 (42, 46, 48, 52) sleeve sts, pick up and knit 3 (4, 4, 4, 4) sts, place marker and join to work in the round—48 (50, 54, 56, 60) sts.

Knit in the round for 1"/2.5 cm.

Dec Rnd: K1, ssk, k to last 3 sts, k2tog, k1—2 sts dec.

Work Dec Rnd every 10 (10, 11, 12, 12) rnds a total of 6 (6, 6, 6, 7) times—36 (38, 42, 44, 46) sts.

Work even until sleeve measures 10.5 (11, 11.75, 13, 14.25)"/27 (28, 30, 33, 36) cm.

Switch to B and smaller needles.

Rib: *K1, p1; rep from * around.

Work in Rib for 2"/5 cm.

BO all sts.

Finishing

COLLAR

Remove provisional CO and place sts on spare needle, ready to work. Starting at right front, pick up and knit 21 (21, 24, 24, 27) sts on vertical edge, pm, knit across 33 (37, 37, 41, 41) neckline sts, pm, pick up and knit 21 (21, 24, 24, 27) sts on left front vertical edge—75 (79, 85, 89, 95) sts.

Rib (WS): *P1, k1; rep from * to last st, p1.
Rib (RS): *K1, p1; rep from * to last st, k1.
Work 5 rows in Rib, ending after a WS row.

Short-Row Shaping

Work in Rib as set, picking up wraps on return rows.
Short Rows 1–2: Work to second marker, W&T, work to marker, W&T.
Short Rows 3–4: Work to wrap, work 4 more sts, W&T, work to wrap, work 4 more sts, W&T.
Work Short Rows 3 –4 a total of 5 times.
Work to end of row. Remove all markers and pick up any remaining wraps on foll row.
Work 5 more rows in Rib, ending after a WS row.
BO with Buttonhole: BO in Rib to last 7 sts. K1 (2 sts on RH needle). Work these 2 sts in I-cord for a total of 5 rows. Resume BO to end of row.

Seam right front collar edge to CO center front sts. Layer left front collar on top of right front collar and sew to attach. Attach button across from BO buttonhole. Weave in all loose ends. Block.

FINISHED MEASUREMENTS

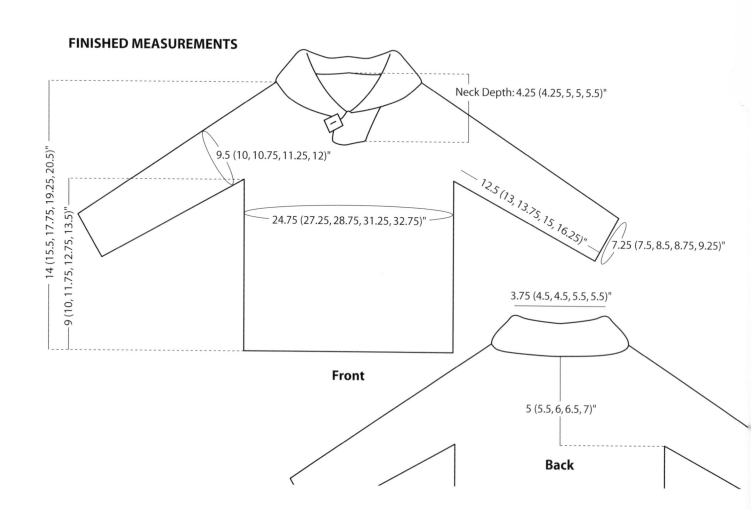

Neck Depth: 4.25 (4.25, 5, 5, 5.5)"

9.5 (10, 10.75, 11.25, 12)"

12.5 (13, 13.75, 15, 16.25)"

14 (15.5, 17.75, 19.25, 20.5)"

9 (10, 11.75, 12.75, 13.5)"

24.75 (27.25, 28.75, 31.25, 32.75)"

7.25 (7.5, 8.5, 8.75, 9.25)"

3.75 (4.5, 4.5, 5.5, 5.5)"

Front

5 (5.5, 6, 6.5, 7)"

Back

Acknowledgments

I am certain I would not have authored this book were it not for the myriad wonderful people that the Lord has been gracious enough with whom to surround me. I have been given the most supportive husband ever who is also an incredible father and an example to all of our little men. Thank you, Ryan, for putting up with the messy house and a lot of takeout—especially while this project was in its final stages. Thank you in advance for continuing to put up with the messy house particularly because, let's face it, housekeeping is not my strong suit.

My dear, sweet boys, Jesse, Charlie, Oliver, and Eliot, are the inspiration behind this book. These poor children don't even know that it's not normal to wear hand knit sweaters in 95-degree weather so that mama can have pictures taken for work! I give a huge thanks to the babysitters, Grandmommy and Nana, who helped to keep my people happy and fed, if not clean, during various photo shoots and writing time, and for their love and devotion to our family always.

Sara Parker is such a talented photographer and I am so lucky to have had her work with me over the past few years, almost from the inception of Tot Toppers. I do not know where my brand would be today were it not for Sara and I will miss her terribly as she is moving away. I thank her for always making time for us.

I am grateful for my friends, Anne and Brantley, who graciously opened their homes for pictures; Mrs. Mitchum on behalf of Pleasant Hill Elementary, and Jesse's first grade teachers, Ms. Hughes and Senorita Hood, for allowing the use of their classrooms. It was so important to me to keep these boys in their natural environments.

I had such a slew of adorable children whose parents let me borrow them for this book. I thank them so much for going out of their way to bring me their kids, dress them up, and most of all for making funny faces, jumping up and down for real smiles, and trying to prevent them from sweating as I failed miserably in my attempt to beat the South Carolina summer heat.

To Kim, Renae, and Joan, who were all so crucial to getting these pieces knit. I am grateful for the millions of questions to make sure the knitting was knit my way, for ripping and redoing when necessary, and for making every single deadline.

The combined influences of great Aunt Dindy and my sister Joey led me to knitting in the first place; Aunt Dindy was the teacher and Joey was the competitive force that first sparked my interest. I also thank them for being willing to proofread this manuscript and provide feedback. Thank you also to Wendy Bernard for being a source of encouragement and another volunteer copy editor.

I appreciate the excitement from Stackpole about this project and the freedom I was given to create the book of my dreams. Thank you to both Kyle Weaver and Candi Derr, my editors, for the positive feedback and expertise that brought this book from my head to paper. Many thanks, also, to my paginator, Wendy Reynolds, and Caroline Stover for creating the schematics.

Thank you to these little men for modeling the items in this book:

Mattox James Bolen
Tucker Allen Bolen
Joseph Henry Crosby
Caden Wei Gissendanner
Jacob Michael Large
Reyburn Benson Lominack
Jesse Ryan Oates, II
Charles Lee Oates
Oliver Henry Oates
Eliot Thatcher Oates
Jacob Speece
Cooper Douglas Stone
Kevin Williams
Charles Edward Winston

Yarn and Notion Sources

The companies below have generously provided support for the knitted samples shown in Knits for Boys. Use their websites to find their wonderful products online, or to find a yarn shop near you that carries their yarn.

Anzula
www.anzula.com

Berroco, Inc.
http://www.berroco.com

Big Bad Wool
http://www.bbwool.com/

Ewe Ewe Yarns
http://www.eweewe.com

Lorna's Laces
http://www.lornaslaces.net

Madelinetosh
http://www.madelinetosh.com

The Plucky Knitter
http://www.thepluckyknitter.com/

Pollika
http://www.pollika.com/

Renaissance/Blue Moon Buttons
http://www.renaissancebuttons.com

Skacel Collection, Inc
http://www.skacelknitting.com

Spud & Chloë
http://www.spudandchloe.com/

Technical Support

If you have a pattern question or are confused about something in the book, you can visit http://www.tottoppers.com for links to frequently asked questions and other resources for support.

These patterns have been scoured and edited and knitted and it is my sincerest hope that they are error free. If however anything does crop up, errata will be listed at: http://www.tottoppers.com/littlemen.

Visual Index